a guide to

PROVENCE

by

WEEKEND JOURNALS

WORDS
Milly Kenny-Ryder

DESIGN
Simon Lovell

PHOTOGRAPHY
Gabriel Kenny-Ryder

weekendjournals.co.uk

CONTENTS

Our chosen places take you on a journey from Arles in the west of Provence to Menton in the east.

Preface	9
Map of Provence	10
HÔTEL DU CLOÎTRE	12
CHARDON	14
LA MAIN QUI PENSE	16
LA CHASSAGNETTE	18
LE CHÂTEAU DES ALPILLES	20
LE BISTROT DU PARADOU	22
MONASTÈRE SAINT-PAUL DE MAUSOLE	24
CQFD	26
LA MAISON PERNOISE	28
SAVONNERIE MARIUS FABRE	30
STUDIO FOTOKINO	32
PÉPÉ	34
CASA ORTEGA	36
MAISON EMPEREUR	38
AM PAR ALEXANDRE MAZZIA	42
CHEZ LUCAS	44
SÉPIA	46
MAGASIN GÉNÉRAL PLUS	48
LES VIEILLES CANAILLES	50
MANA ESPRESSO	52
POINTE NOIRE	54

ATELIER DE CÉZANNE	56
BASTIDE	60
CHÂTEAU & VILLA LA COSTE	62
CHÂTEAU BARBEBELLE	66
LA BASTIDE DE GORDES	68
SCARAMOUCHE	72
LA BASTIDE DE MOUSTIERS	74
CHÂTEAU DE BERNE	76
LE RELAIS DES MOINES	78
CHÂTEAU SAINTE-ROSELINE	80
MUSÉE DE L'ANNONCIADE	82
PAN DEÏ PALAIS	84
RONDINI, SANDALES TROPÉZIENNES	86
HÔTEL LES ROCHES ROUGES	88
L'USINE HISTORIQUE, LES PARFUMERIES FRAGONARD	94
FONDATION MARGUERITE ET AIMÉ MAEGHT	96
MUSÉE PICASSO	98
CAP MODERNE	100
MIRAZUR	104
An Interview with Frédéric Fekkai	108
An Interview with Madeleine Herbeau	112
An Interview with Jamie Beck	116
An Interview with Mauro Colagreco	120
Further Ideas	124

PREFACE

It is easy to fall in love with Provence. From the moment you step off the plane, the warm air hits you carrying the aroma of sun-baked herbs and salty sea. There is a reason why so many great modern artists settled here, eager to capture the earthy hues, unruly landscapes and crisp, golden light.

For my family it is a second home, a special part of the world which, thanks to my grandmother's heritage and hospitality, is the backdrop to the most magical memories... cracking pine kernels from the forest, playing pétanque at sunset and spotting wild boars after dark.

Researching this book has led to new discoveries, beyond the local markets and picnic spots of my childhood. We travelled as far west as Arles and along the coast eastwards to Menton, the border with Italy. Along the way, past magnificent mountains, vineyards and forests, we found hotels that exude Riviera style, small town restaurants serving classic Provençal cuisine and museums and shops preserving and presenting the essence of the region.

There is so much history behind the glamorous face of modern day Provence. Allow yourself to slow down... find a sleepy café, lovely candlemaker or artisan pottery; settle at a shady table in a village square and enjoy a glass of icy rosé; or enjoy the countryside, the heady pine-scented Provençal air and the crickets' song.

Milly Kenny-Ryder

HÔTEL DU CLOÎTRE

Hotel

18 rue du Cloître, 13200 Arles
+33 (0)4 88 09 10 00
hotelducloitre.com

There is something instantly enchanting about the location of this quirky boutique hotel in Arles. Tucked away at the top of a winding road and concealed by the shadow of a 100-year old Paulownia tree, Hôtel du Cloître is a fairytale location for a weekend away.

As you walk into this hotel you are instantly greeted with wacky, eye-catching clashes of colour and pattern paired with old-fashioned interiors. It is the signature look from designer India Mahdavi. There are 19 rooms at Hôtel du Cloître, each arranged and decorated in a similar style with statement headboards and magnificent psychedelic tiled bathrooms. Downstairs, the lime yellow living room is a lovely setting for breakfast.

Next door to the hotel, in a cobbled stone square, is the delightful little L'Ouvre Boite restaurant, perfect for a light tapas lunch or early evening drink.

CHARDON

Restaurant

37 rue des Arènes, 13200 Arles
+33 (0)9 72 86 72 04
hellochardon.com

The pop-up concept is not well known in the South of France, but when the successful trio Laura Vidal (from Frenchie in Paris), Harry Cummins (a British chef) and Julia Vidal (a Québécoise sommelier) arrived from their hit Parisian pop-up venture, they were sure to make a success of their newest idea in Arles.

Chardon opened in the summer of 2016, a creative eatery showcasing the culinary skills of renowned visiting chefs. The cosy and artistic venue is a lovely place to visit for lunch or dinner after exploring the galleries in town. The walls are decorated with trinkets and memories, and mismatched plates add extra character.

Chefs travel from far and wide to cook in the Chardon kitchen, each devising a concise but exciting list of dishes to surprise and delight guests. Chef residencies have included Deborah Blank (from Ester in Sydney) and Tomas Scarpetti (who works with Francis Mallman). The menu is always made up of small plates designed for sharing and they recommend you order one of everything, a generous feeding for a table of two.

Chardon offers a rare opportunity to try exotic and intriguing flavours not often found in the kitchens of Provence.

LA MAIN QUI PENSE

Shop

15 rue tour de Fabre, 13200 Arles
+33 (0)4 90 18 24 58
cecilecayrol.com

Tucked away in the charming cobbled streets of Arles, La Main Qui Pense is a humble pottery studio and shop. Potter Cécile Cayrol's quaint little atelier suits the backdrop of Arles' old town.

Cécile is a native Arlésienne whose interest in ceramics began from a young age when she found ancient Roman pottery shards in her garden. As soon as she was old enough she went to train at the prestigious Vallarius school as an apprentice.

La Main Qui Pense translates as 'The Hand That Thinks' and is home to her workshop as well as exhibiting a small collection of her elegant pieces.

Cécile also teaches pottery classes by appointment.

LA CHASSAGNETTE

Restaurant

Route du Sambuc, 13200 Arles
+33 (0)4 90 97 26 96
chassagnette.fr

La Chassagnette celebrates the abundance of Provençal produce. Set in the idyllic Camargue countryside, 15 miles from the centre of Arles, this is a destination restaurant definitely worth the journey.

Chef Armand Arnal gets much of his inspiration from the bountiful garden that surrounds the restaurant. Here they grow every imaginable fruit, vegetable and herb, ensuring that all the food is organic, aromatic and vibrant. Armand also insists on only using fish and meat indigenous to the area.

Wander around the fragrant garden before settling down at an al fresco table for lunch. In the evening a mosquito-free dining room allows guests to dine outdoors in peace!

Despite its Michelin starred status, La Chassagnette is a relaxed and modest place to eat. And although meat and fish do often feature on the tasting menus, it is the vegetarian dishes that really shine here.

LE CHÂTEAU DES ALPILLES

Hotel

Route de Rougadou, 13210 Saint-Rémy-de-Provence
+33 (0)4 90 92 03 33
chateaudesalpilles.com

A grand, tree lined drive leads to Le Château des Alpilles, an idyllic 19th century manor house hotel on the outskirts of Saint-Rémy-de-Provence. The façade twinkles in the sunlight; the dusty blue shutters and shaded terrace make it the most perfect Provençal scene. A 400 year-old cypress tree in the grounds of the house suggests that the domaine dates back to late medieval times.

There are 21 rooms and suites, of which the 14 in the main house are the most traditional and special. The remaining rooms, located in the old farmhouse, chapel and washhouse, are more modern in style. The hotel's living spaces have a lavish feel, with plenty of velvet and decorative antique furniture adding more than a touch of luxury.

Despite the smart interiors, the hotel has a relaxed ambience, particularly at the swimming pool and bar area. The hotel chef, Mathias Bettinger, has worked at Le Château des Alpilles for over 20 years, serving traditional regional cuisine and classic French dishes.

LE BISTROT DU PARADOU

Restaurant

57 avenue de la Vallée des Baux, 13520 Paradou,
near Saint-Rémy-de-Provence
+33 (0)4 90 54 32 70

This relaxed bistro in Paradou, a quiet village in the west of Provence, is a favourite for those living in and visiting the area.

The building was previously a post office, opening as a restaurant in 1984. Inside, the old-fashioned décor documents the history of the eatery and its famous clientele. The current owners took the reins in 2010 and continue to satisfy customers with hearty fare and friendly service.

There is a fixed main dish for each day of the week, featuring comfort food delights such as aioli, spit-roast Bresse chicken and homemade tarts. The set menu comprises three courses plus an excellent regional cheese board, definitely worth saving space for.

Reservations are essential, particularly at the weekend when many families gather for their weekly meal together.

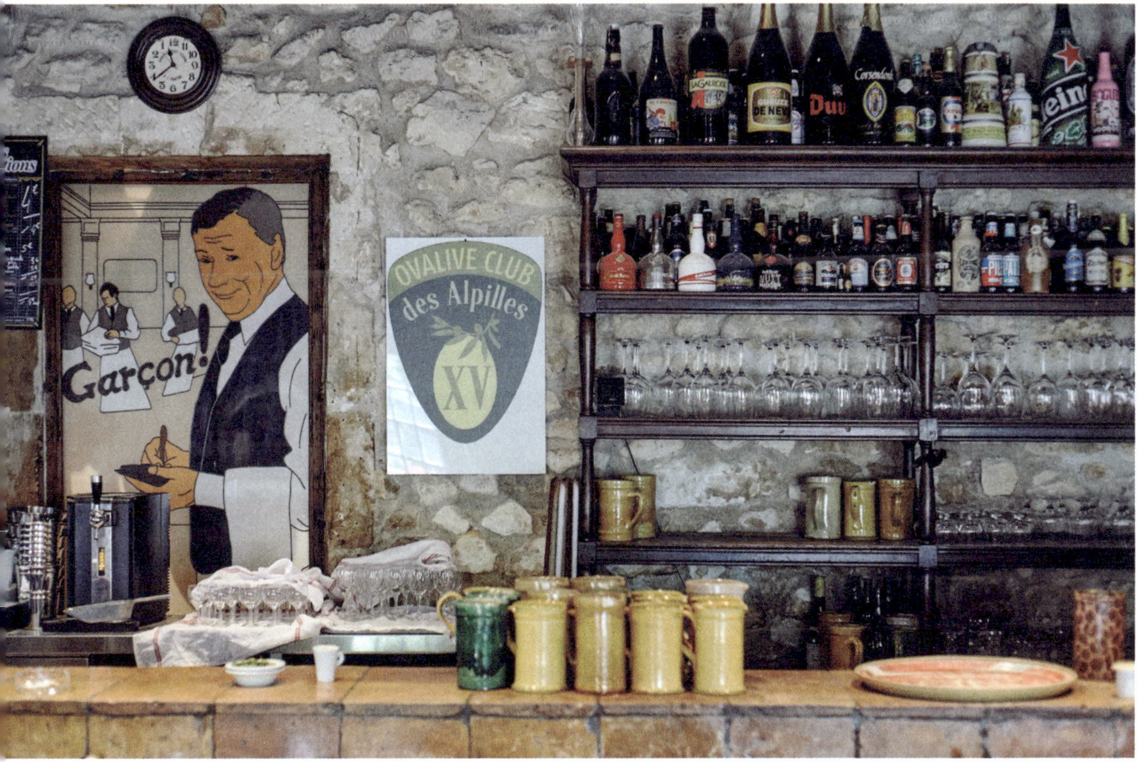
Garçon!
OVALIVE CLUB
des Alpilles
XV

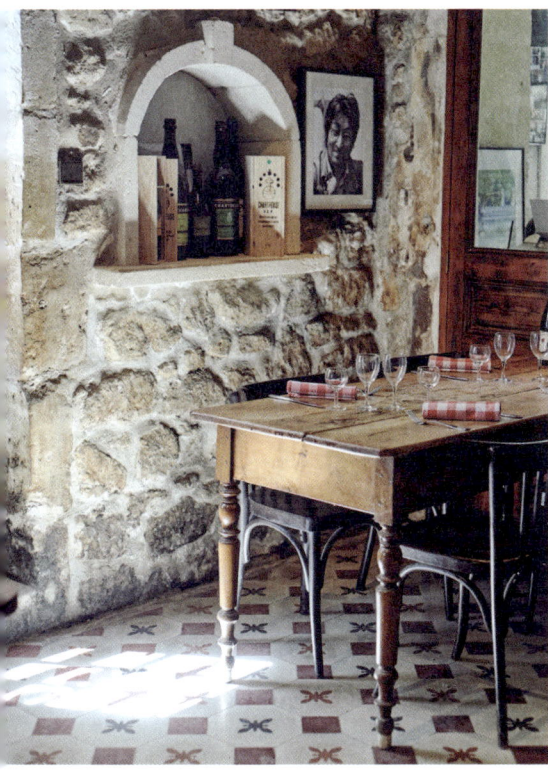

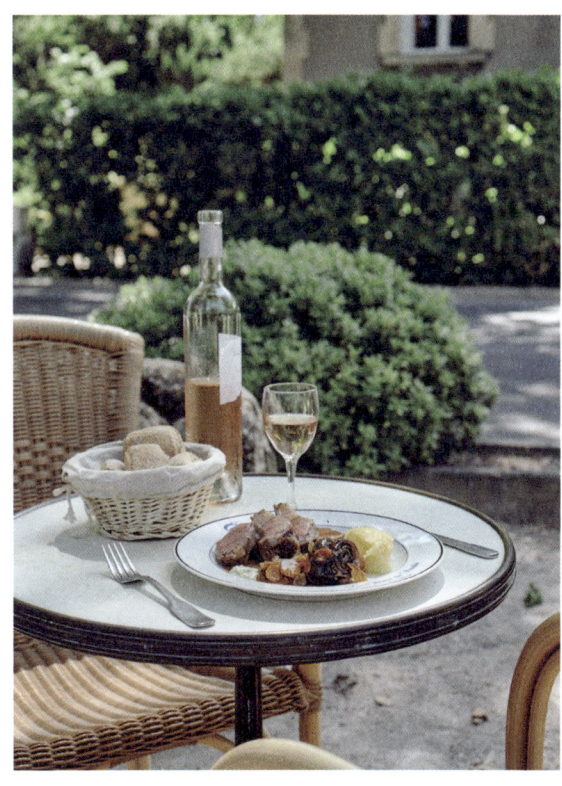

MONASTÈRE SAINT-PAUL DE MAUSOLE

Museum

Avenue Vincent Van Gogh, 13210 Saint-Rémy-de-Provence
+ 33 (0)4 90 92 77 00
saintpauldemausole.fr

When Vincent van Gogh had a nervous breakdown in 1889 he checked himself into the Saint-Paul Asylum and spent six months painting and recuperating.

The psychiatric hospital is still in operation today, but art lovers can visit the historic monastery, the wheat field that Van Gogh painted and a reconstruction of the room where he stayed. The monastery itself is a beautiful example of the Provençal Romanesque style, with 12th century cloisters and an atmospheric chapel. Inside, the white stone offers a quiet place for reflection, and there is a wonderful sense of calm.

Although there are no original Van Gogh paintings on show, visitors can admire 20 large scale reproductions of the artist's works created at the monastery.

CQFD

Shop

16 place de la Principale, 84000 Avignon
+33 (0)4 90 85 29 86
cqfd-avignon.fr

This quirky little shop in Avignon proudly offers a range of homeware, accessories and stationery, all made and designed in France. The owners hope to draw attention to the quality and heritage of French products, with a particular focus on eco-friendly and recycled materials.

The colourful and crowded store is a fun one-stop destination for local and patriotic gifts to take home. For Provençal specific products, La Belle Meche is a lovely brand of scented candles made by hand in Grasse, and Fabrication Française make beautifully crafted woollen knitted bowties in nearby Aix-en-Provence.

For classic French garments, Armor Lux make a range of striped Breton tops, and Bonne Maison is unbeatable for luxurious patterned socks.

LA MAISON PERNOISE

Shop

167 avenue de la Gare, 84210 Pernes les Fontaines, near Avignon
+33 (0)9 81 45 04 22
lamaisonpernoise.com

It takes a little while to find this concept store, which is located in the small town of Pernes les Fontaines just outside Avignon, and once you discover it you will need a few hours to fully examine each and every artefact inside.

In 2013, Lau Dejente opened La Maison Pernoise in a giant converted barn. The store offers a variety of homeware and fashion. It is difficult to know where to look as impressive carpets hang from the banisters and bold posters adorn the walls. Every corner displays a treasure trove of artisan products, carefully chosen for their unique design and functionality.

Items here are both practical and beautiful. Particularly alluring are the ceramics by Jars and natural hemp garments by Couleur Chanvre.

There is also a second branch in Montpellier - Marché du Lez.

where do you
want to spend
eternity ?

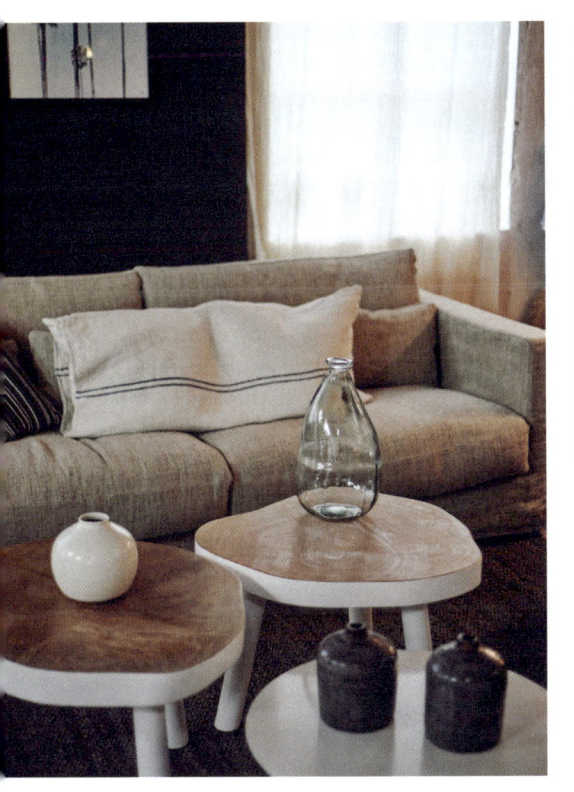

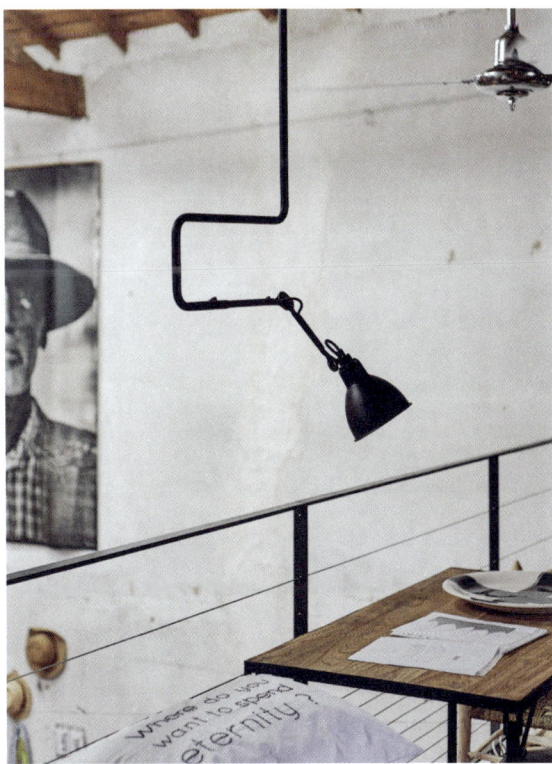

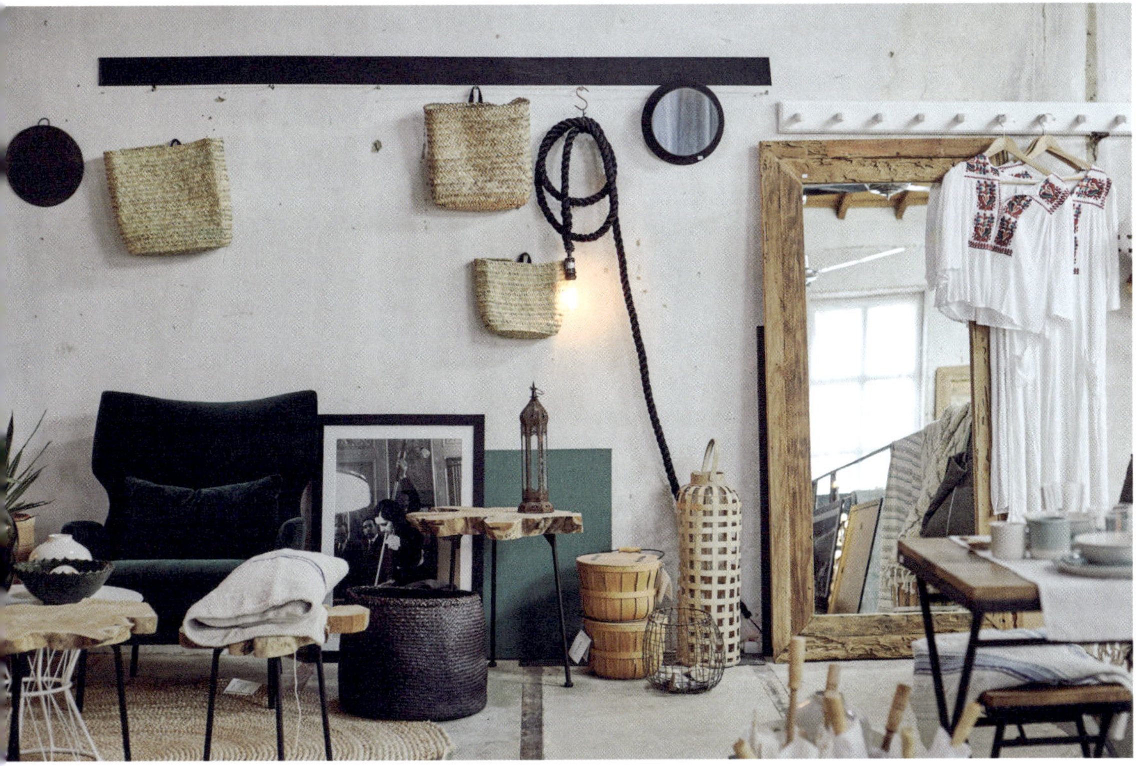

SAVONNERIE MARIUS FABRE

Museum

148 avenue Paul Bourret, 13300 Salon-de-Provence
+33 (0)4 90 53 82 75
marius-fabre.com

Soap is a quintessential Provençal product. It is thanks to the abundance of raw materials like olive oil, soda and salt that Provence is such a successful place for soap manufacture.

In 1900, at the age of 22, Marius Fabre founded his (now renowned) soap company in a garden shed in Salon-de-Provence. In 1927 the Savonnerie moved to its current premises where visitors are able to enjoy a tour. It is Marius' great granddaughters, Marie and Julie Bousquet-Fabre, who run the company now, more than 100 years since its humble beginnings.

The fascinating factory and atmospheric museum tell the family's story and provide an educational background about the process behind this special product. The soap is made from 100% natural materials and is gentle but effective. The factory's shop offers a range of traditional, authentic soaps to buy and take home.

STUDIO FOTOKINO

Gallery

33 Allées Gambetta, 13001 Marseille
+33 (0)9 81 65 26 44
fotokino.org

The modest entrance to Studio Fotokino indicates little about what is inside this quirky Marseille gallery. The non-profit organisation was started in 2000 as a social and community enterprise to showcase visual arts. A bright white gallery holds temporary exhibitions of illustration, graphic design, cinema, photography and painting. Artists who have shown their work here in the past include illustrators Paul Cox and Kitty Crowther, as well as designers Fredun Shapur and Nathalie Du Pasquier.

The space is free to visit and welcomes all, adults and children. You can also purchase a print as a memento of your visit from the bookshop.

Fotokino host workshops and talks throughout the year inside the studio and around town. Their 'La Bibliocyclette' serves the local community with a library-on-a-bike service.

PÉPÉ

Restaurant

15 cours Julien, 13006 Marseille
+33 (0)7 81 02 21 47

This neighbourhood restaurant is found on the lively cours Julien, a trendy street in the east of Marseille populated by hip eateries, bars and independent boutiques. Palm trees shade the streets and the walls are covered in colourful graffiti. The area comes to life at sunset when people crowd the wide pavements enjoying good food and wine.

Pépé opened in early 2017 as the second venue for Jérôme Benoît, chef-owner of well established Marseille restaurant Mémé. It is run by Tanguy Bacrot, while Jérôme's protégé, Stanislas Clavier, heads up the kitchen. A pale pink neon sign indicates the whereabouts of this popular establishment, and inside, vintage furniture and ornate wallpaper set the scene and encourage diners to unwind.

The seasonal menu focuses on meat and shellfish, and the indulgent but casual dishes are perfect for group feasting.

CASA ORTEGA

Guesthouse

46 rue des Petites Maries, 13001 Marseille
+33 (0)6 80 62 53 21
casa-ortega.fr

Legend has it that Casa Ortega was once the hideout for the famous gypsy castanets player, Juan Sebastián Ortega. After falling in love with a forbidden young girl in Argentina, they eloped to this house in Marseille. Within a few years the building became a meeting place for well-known musicians and artists; there are rumours that Picasso and Hemingway were seen here.

The pale green tiled exterior is striking among the rustic surrounding buildings. Everyone who passes by is intrigued by what goes on behind the black door of 46 rue des Petites Maries. Those in the know come to stay at Casa Ortega, Marseille's most surprising and cosy guesthouse.

The interior exudes personality and flair. The five psychedelic rooms are decorated individually with retro 20th century furnishings and dazzling patterned wallpaper from UK brand Graham & Brown. The top green bedroom is perhaps the most desirable, but all the rooms have their own seductive quirks.

Casa Ortega is reasonably priced, the service is very friendly and the staff will help you navigate your way to the city's best haunts.

MAISON EMPEREUR

Shop & Apartment

4 rue des Récolettes, 13001 Marseille
+33 (0)4 91 54 02 29
empereur.fr

Maison Empereur is a Marseille institution, a wondrous and endless hardware store that dates back to 1827. It is a collector's paradise: practical, aesthetic and poetic. The shop is full of variety with every cooking utensil or household contrivance you could ever need or want. If you have discovered an old treasure in a local antique market, it is likely you will find a lovely modern version here. Next door to the main store is an additional Maison Empereur shop selling a range of Mont St Michel sweaters and real Camargue boots.

For an extra special stay in Marseille, book a night at the Maison Empereur apartment. This guesthouse is a magical place to rest your head, a museum of the shop's precious memorabilia and archived artefacts. There is a comforting sense of tradition as you walk through the door, reinforced by the beautiful old bed, authentic wooden bathtub and original kitchen fittings.

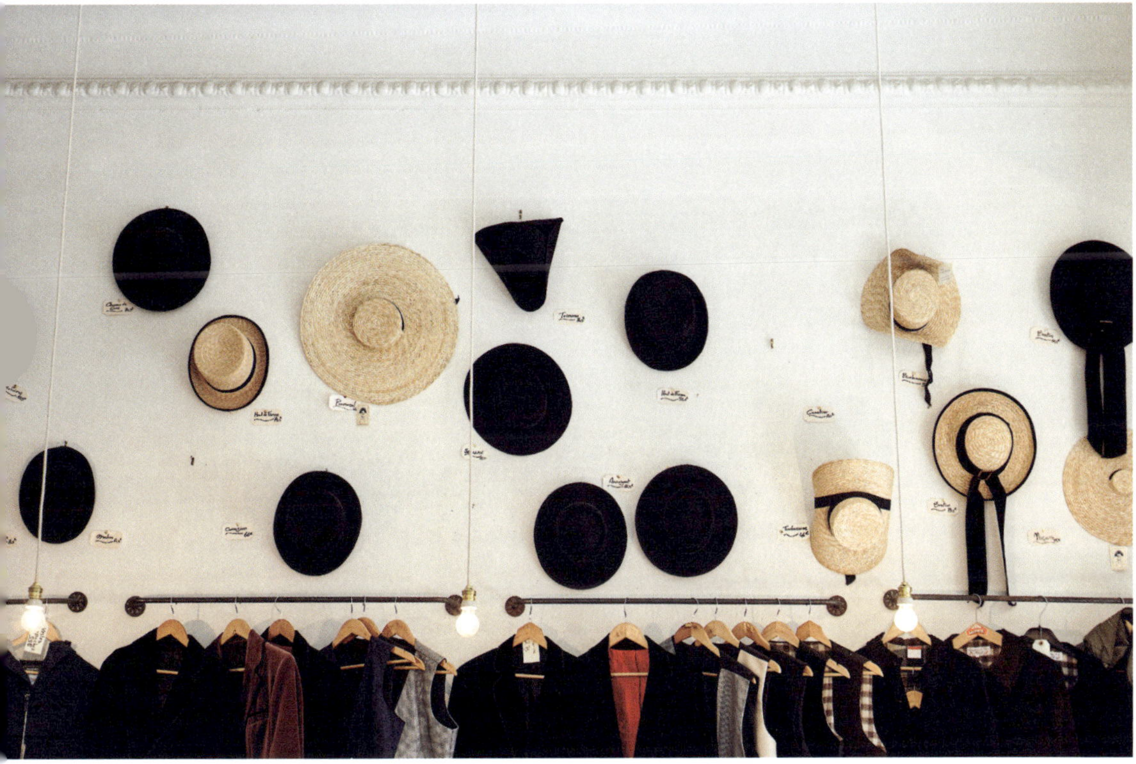

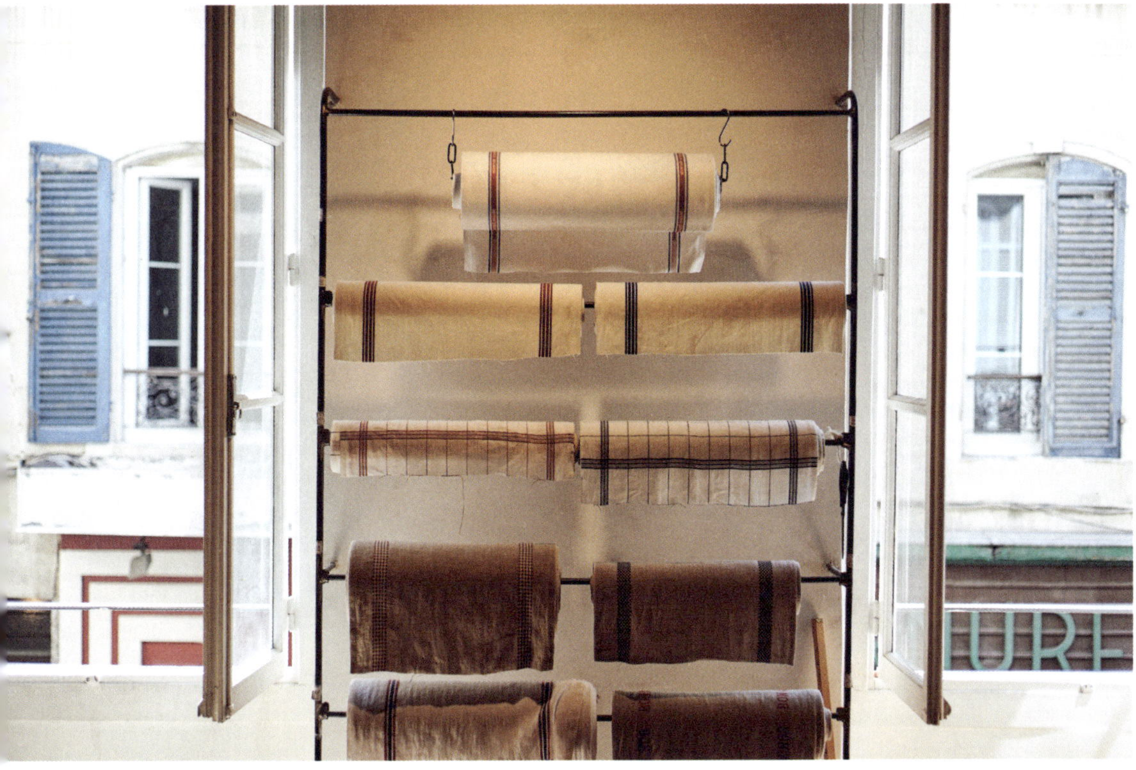

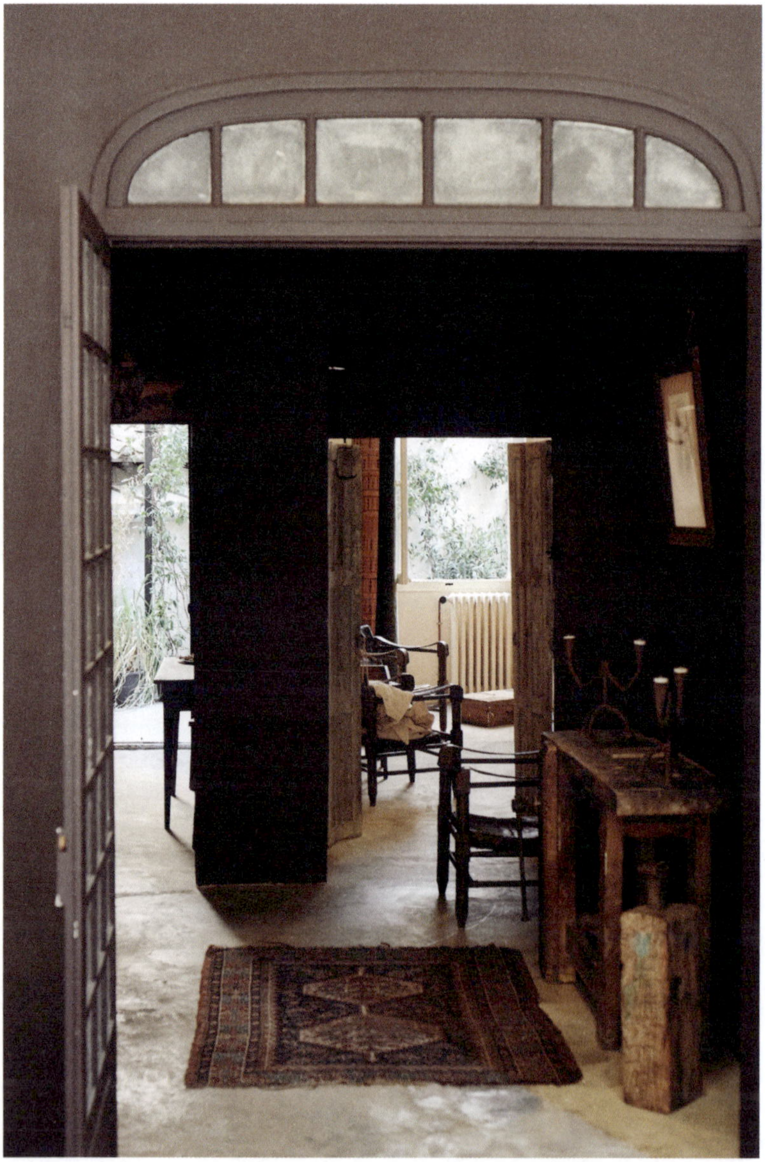

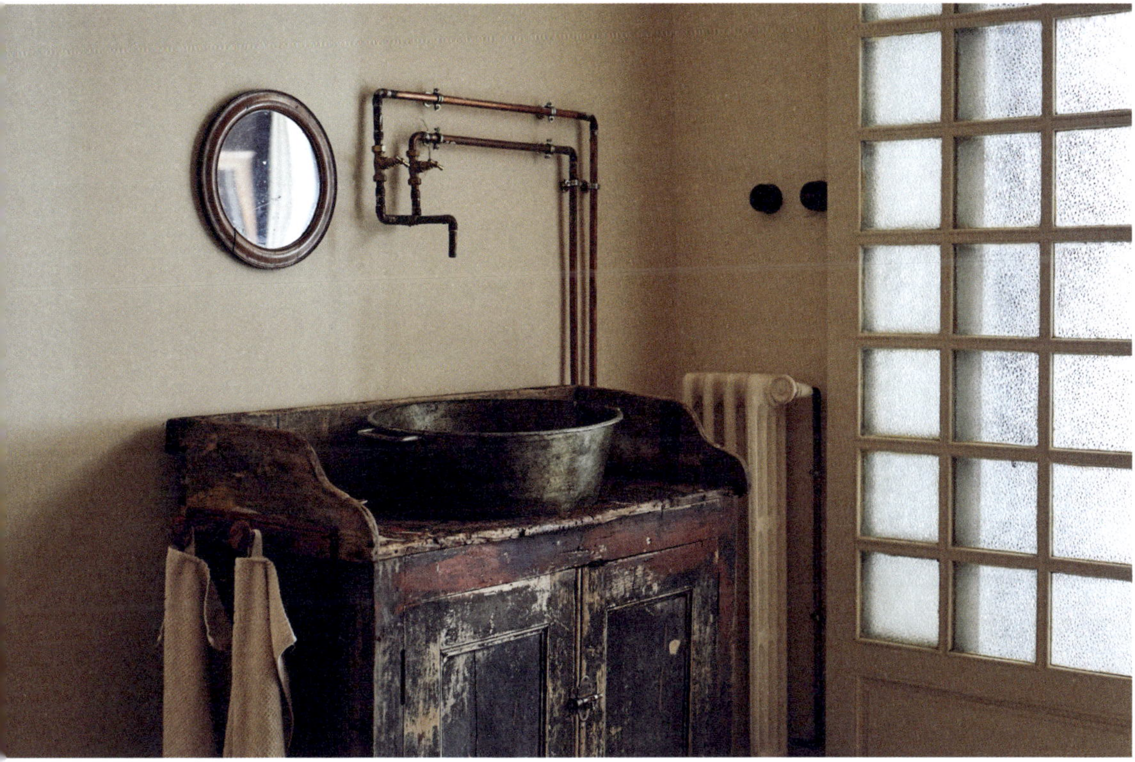

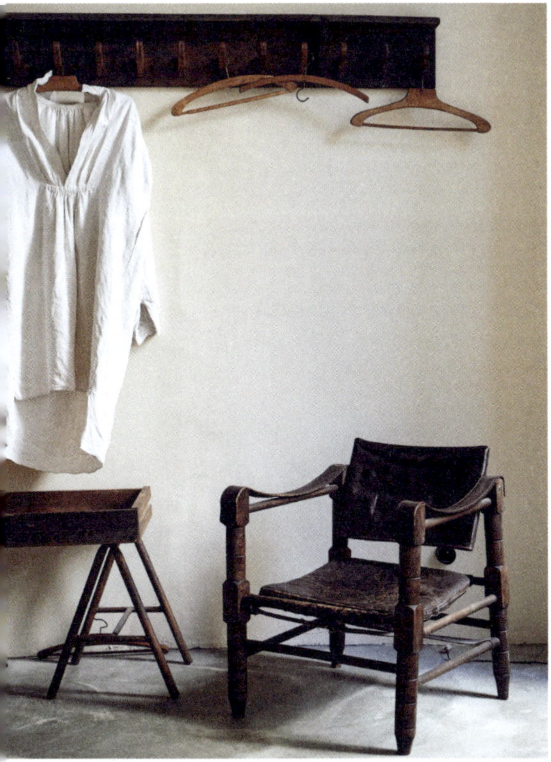

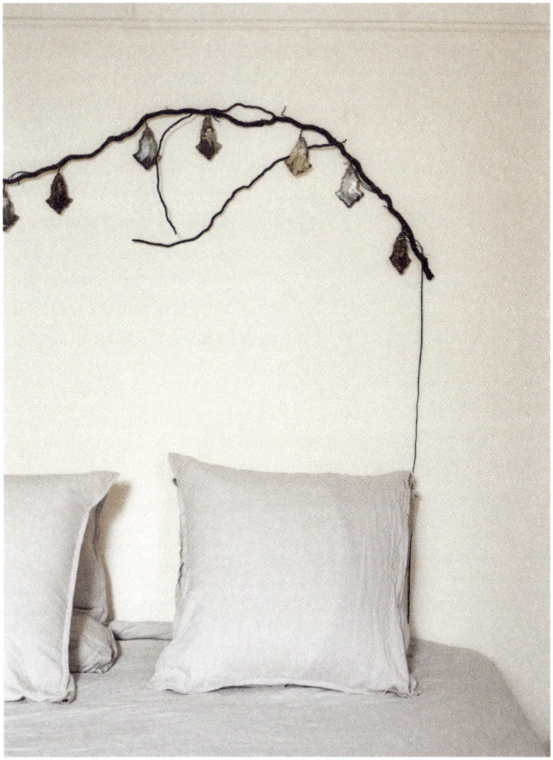

AM PAR ALEXANDRE MAZZIA

Restaurant

9 rue François Rocca, 13008 Marseille
+33 (0)4 91 24 83 63
alexandremazzia.com

There is no doubt about it, Alexandre Mazzia has brought a new dimension of culinary excellence to Marseille.

This highly regarded chef's first solo restaurant is found on the outskirts, in a residential part of town. The petite and chic, minimalist dining room seats just 22 people, plus two extra coveted bar places with an exclusive view of the kitchen. The interiors are modern and stylish with simple blonde oak tables and textured concrete walls.

Alexandre creates thought provoking and palate thrilling food through a series of small delicate dishes. There is no menu, diners simply choose a number of courses and pay accordingly. Lunch is a brilliant way to taste Alexandre's exquisite and sensitive cuisine at an affordable price.

Particularly memorable are the initial miniature snacks, immaculate little works of art assembled from unusual combinations of the finest ingredients.

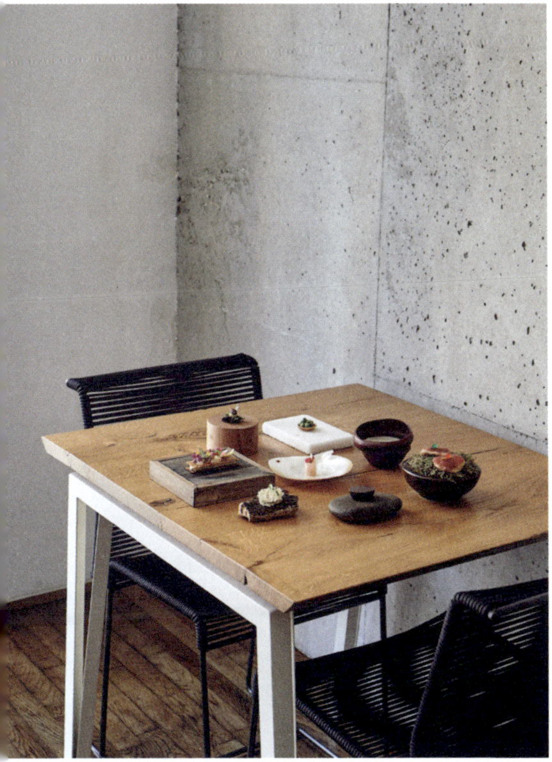
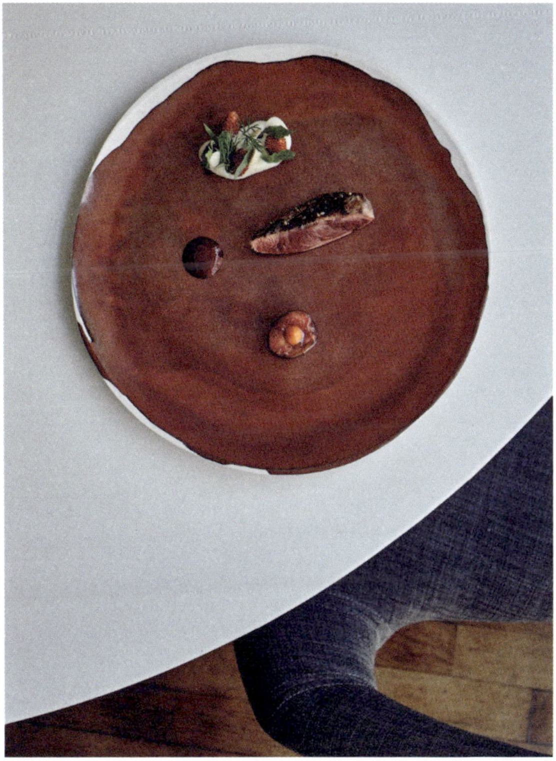
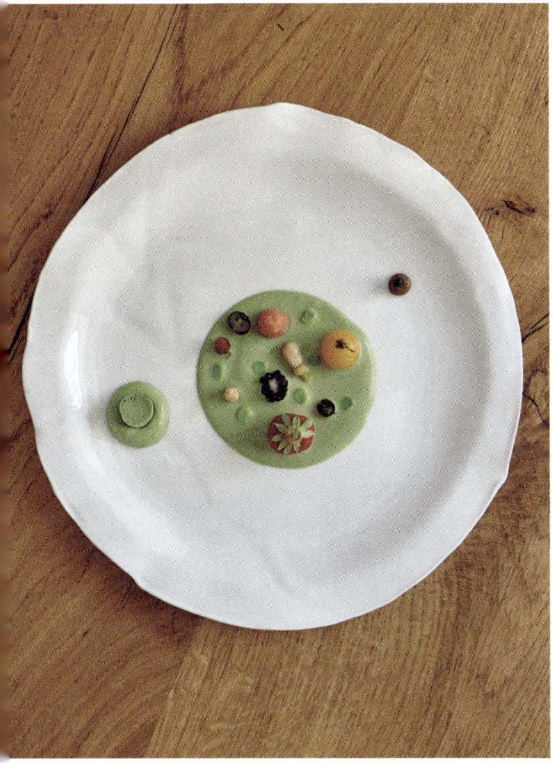
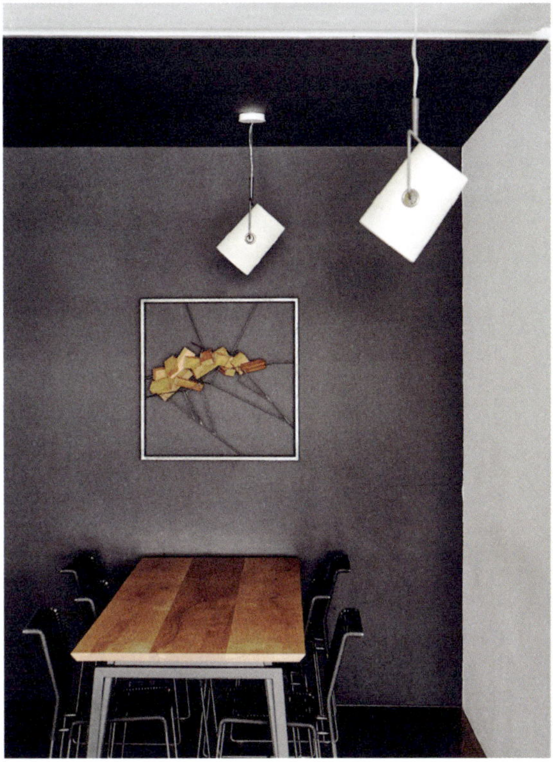

CHEZ LUCAS

Shop

56 rue des Moulins, 13002 Marseille
chezlucas.fr

Rue du Panier is perhaps the most picturesque road in Marseille's old town. The steep street is home to many cute cafés and eye-catching shops, but you'll have to weave your way through the snapping tourists.

Just off the main street, Chez Lucas is a beautiful mess of forgotten French relics and antiques. Owner, Lucas, has created an eclectic emporium of recycled vintage treasures that he has lovingly collected from markets and fairs from all over the region. The emotional connection he has with his items is clear and many objects have amazing stories that Lucas will happily share with you.

Pick up a one-of-a-kind Provençal piece, from a 1950s school poster to a pretty Pastis jug or a decorative old clock.

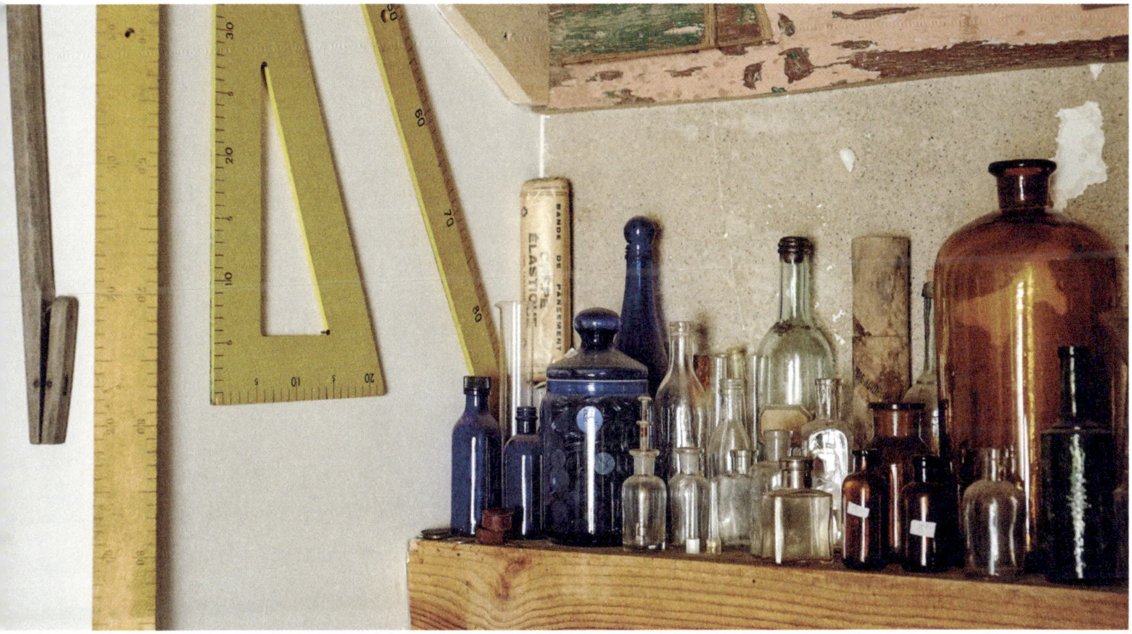

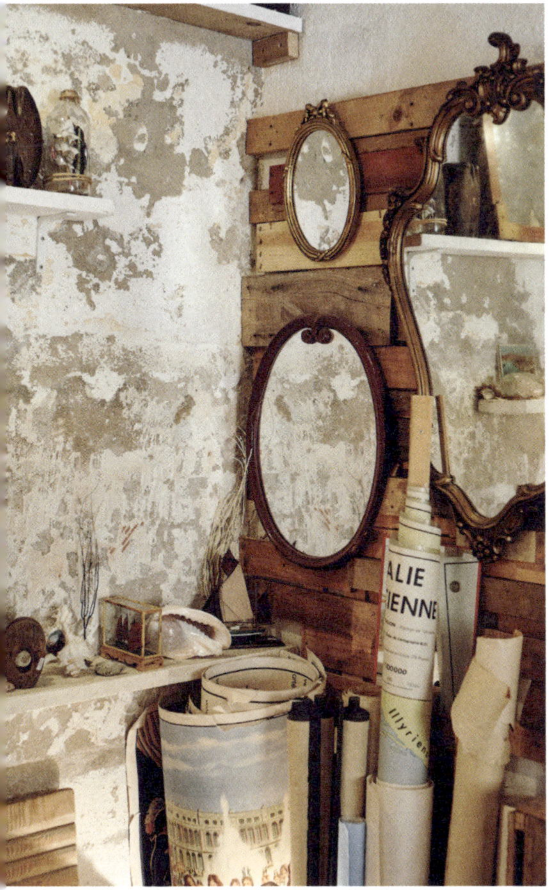

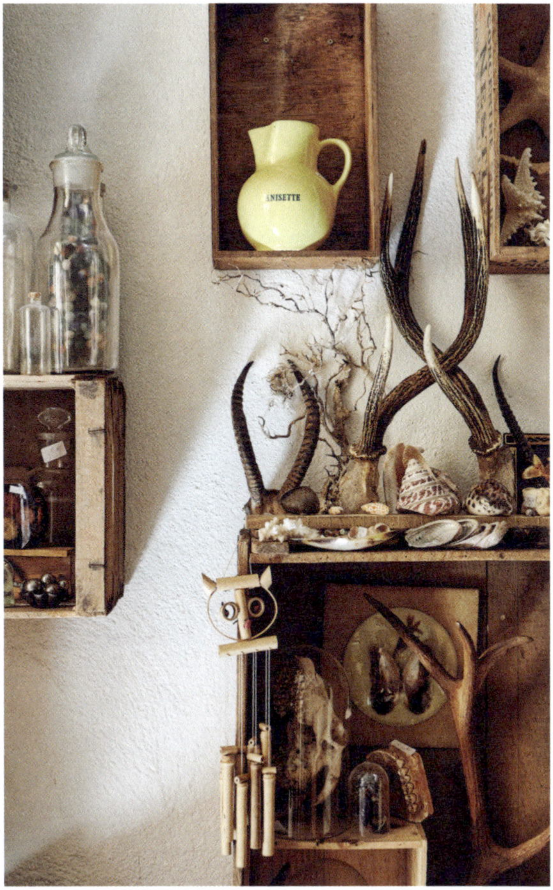
ANISETTE

SÉPIA

Restaurant

2 rue Vauvenargues, 13007 Marseille
+33 (0)9 83 82 67 27

For destination dining in Marseille, Sépia is one of the most spectacular options. This stylish eatery is found at the top of Jardin Pierre Puget, the oldest garden in the city. The views are breathtaking and the atmosphere is infectious.

After a steep walk through the park you will be more than ready to relax on the terrace with a glass of wine. The dining room inside is stylish, with simple design features and large windows.

Chef Paul Langlère is from Marseille but has a wealth of experience from working further afield in some of Europe's top kitchens. His menu at Sépia follows the seasons and champions market specialities. In the winter a variety of creative bistro-style dishes are on offer. In the warmer months Paul particularly utilises the restaurant's vegetable garden to create fresher, lighter cuisine.

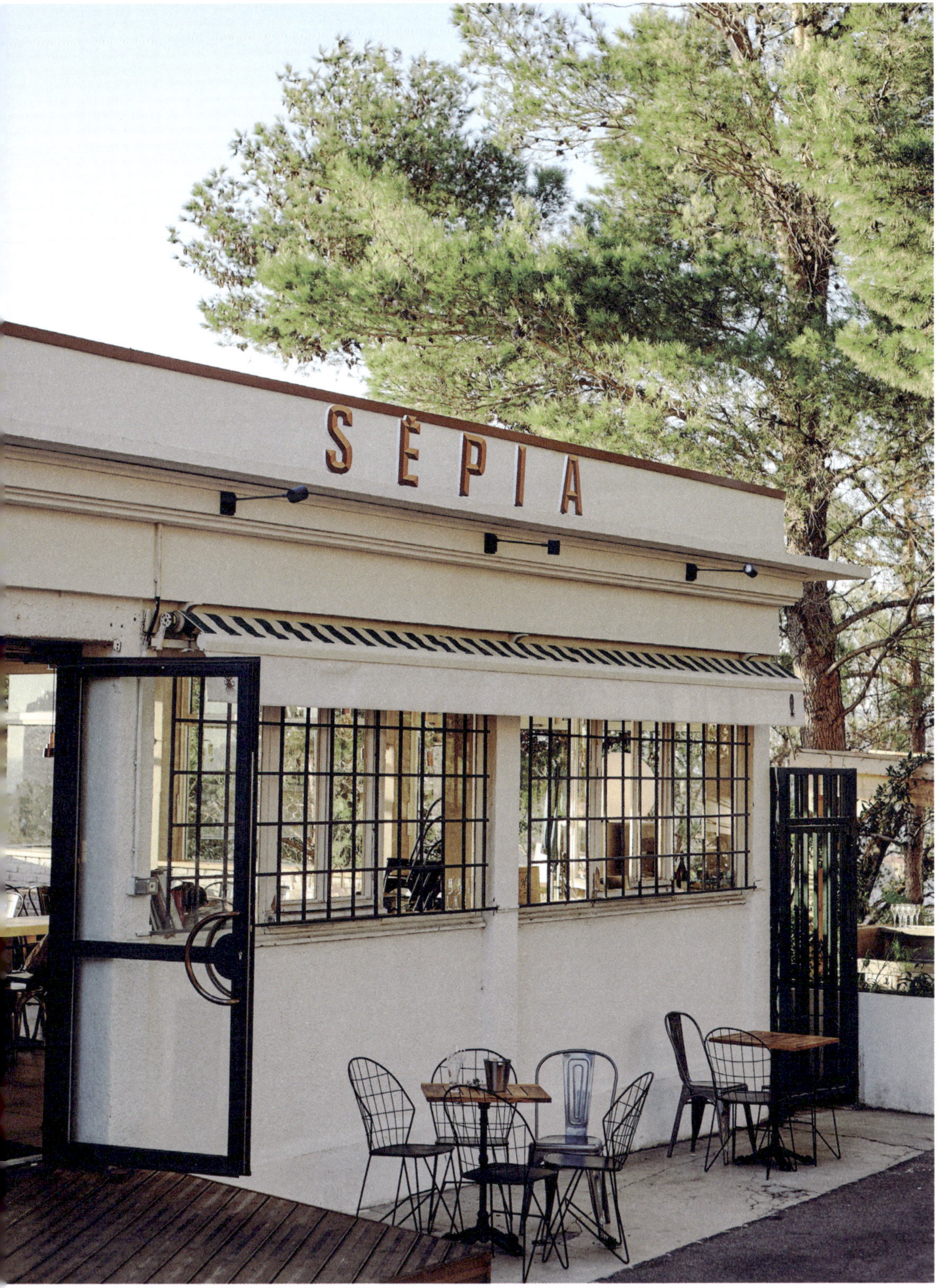
SÉPIA

MAGASIN GÉNÉRAL PLUS

Shop

3/5 rue Matheron, 13100 Aix-en-Provence
+33 (0)4 42 21 97 14
novoidplus.com

Magasin Général Plus is one of three lifestyle stores in Aix-en-Provence opened by a trio of brothers. This shop is found on the sleepy rue Matheron and is surrounded by several other delightful boutiques.

You will need plenty of time to explore and examine the eclectic mix of objects in-store. The brothers aim to sell an assortment of nostalgic and fun items inspired by their passions – fashion, music and travelling. Stock up on hip French gifts to take home such as pétanque balls from La Boule Belle, modern Marseille soaps by La Corvette and high quality Opinel wooden-handled knives, which have been made in Saint-Jean-de-Maurienne since 1890.

Their two other concept stores sell different collections and are worth visiting if you are in town. Novoid Plus offers men's apparel, footwear, and accessories while their third outlet, Motto, is a collaboration with Carhartt that opened in 2015.

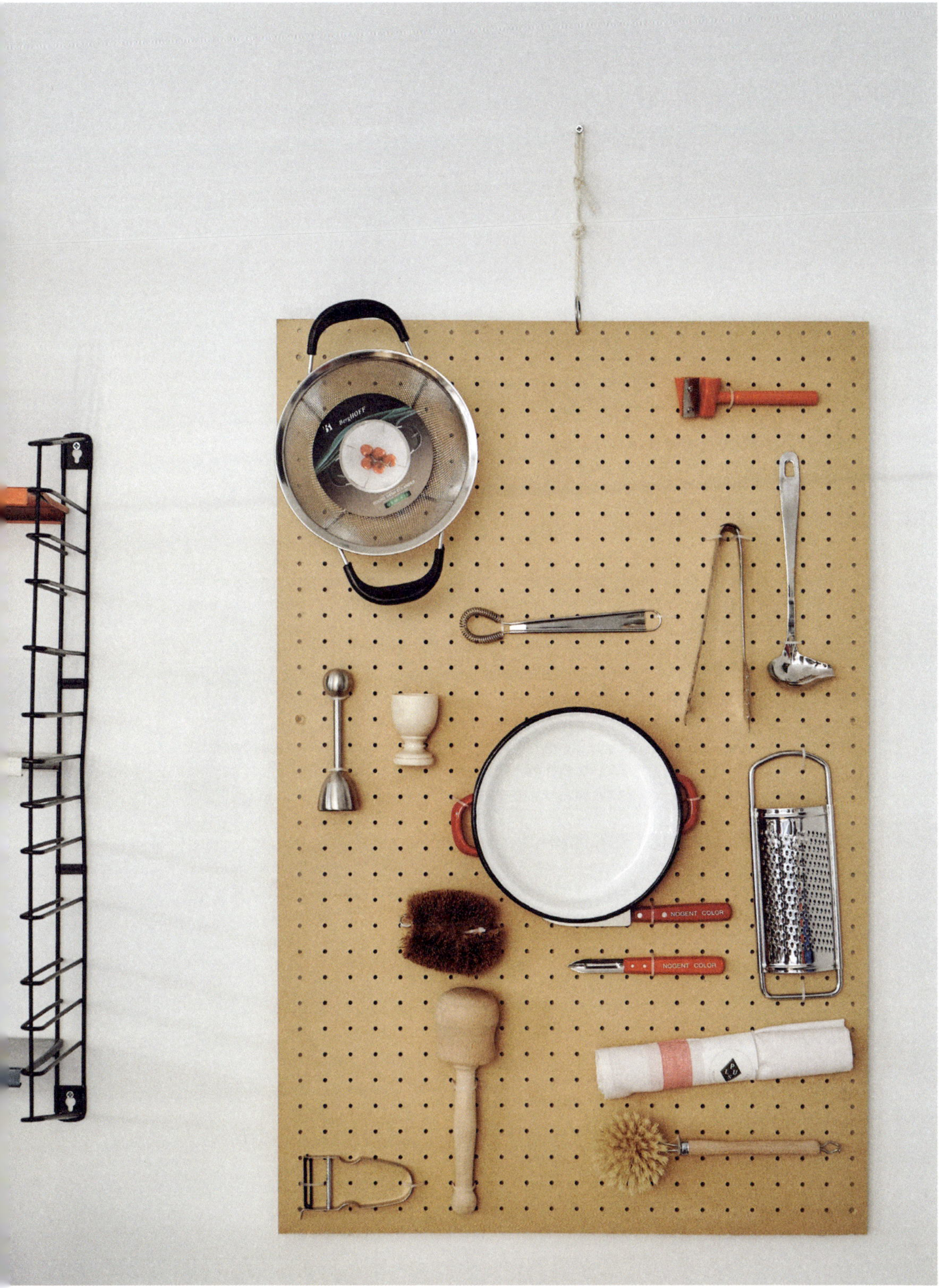
BergHOFF
NOGENT COLOR
NOGENT COLOR

LES VIEILLES CANAILLES

Restaurant

7 rue Isolette, 13100 Aix-en-Provence
+33 (0)4 42 91 41 75
vieilles-canailles.fr

Les Vieilles Canailles represents the best of French bistro dining. This Aix-en-Provence eatery is friendly and unpretentious, with simple décor and great classic French food.

Chef Pierre Hochard handpicks ingredients from local farmers to ensure he is using the freshest produce. The restaurant is small with just a handful of tables and his kitchen space is even smaller. The menu changes daily, but you can expect to see a range of inventive salads and refined meat and fish dishes. At lunchtime there is a reasonably priced set menu, which allows you to try three courses for less than €30.

The wine list, personally chosen by Pierre, focuses on red and white wine, rather than the usual Provençal rosé. His knowledgeable waiters can help you choose a wine to match your menu choices perfectly.

Polugar
JANOT
Le Canard enchaîné
Macron : "J'ai plus d'une corde à monarque !"
Verdict de la Cour des comptes : un trou de 9 milliards dans le budget 2017
Les nouvelles surprises du système Ferrand

ÉMILE ET ROSE, 2014 .... 20€

MANA ESPRESSO

Café

12 rue des Bernardines, 13100 Aix-en-Provence
manaespresso.fr

It may be a while before speciality coffee is properly established in Southern France but there are a few trendsetters beginning to pave the way.

Mana Espresso is found down a quiet street in Aix-en-Provence. The modestly designed café was founded by couple Benjamin and Alex, who met while studying in Paris. After working in several eateries in the capital they decided to bring their love of good coffee to the south. The small café has eight tables inside and a bench out the front where you can enjoy your drink in the sun. They serve the best beans from around the world (origins and varieties change with the seasons). The coffee is carefully roasted and perfectly poured.

Those in the know stop by for a light vegan breakfast or a much needed caffeine refuel in between shopping stints.

GALA
FESTIVAL
VICTOIRE
CAFÉS
MORNING SIP
COFFEE
COFFEE-POT

POINTE NOIRE
—
Restaurant

37 place des Tanneurs, 13100 Aix-en-Provence
+33 (0)4 42 92 71 35
pointenoire.fr

Brothers Jean-Laurent and Alexandre Mazzia are making quite a name for themselves in Provence. Alexandre is the chef mastermind behind Michelin celebrated AM in Marseille, and Jean-Laurent runs Pointe Noire, a more relaxed culinary destination in Aix-en-Provence.

The Scandinavian-inspired décor at Pointe Noire stands out against the rustic cafés of Aix. Spacious and chic, it is a pleasant place to sit for a meal anytime of the day.

The kitchen produces gourmet tapas, ideal for sharing as a group. The recipes are evocative and experimental, and the price dependent on the number of plates you choose.

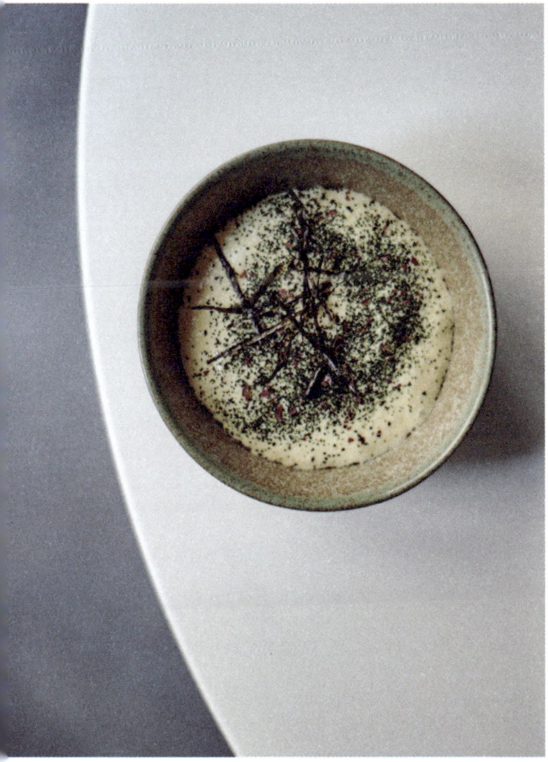

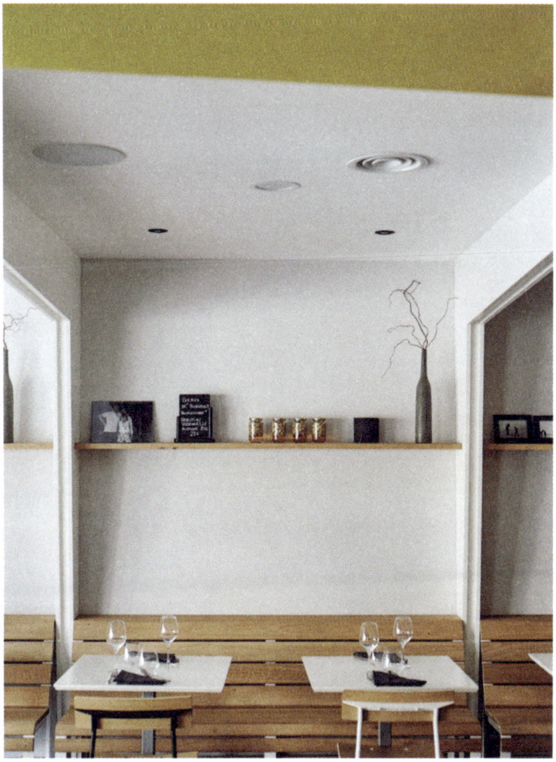

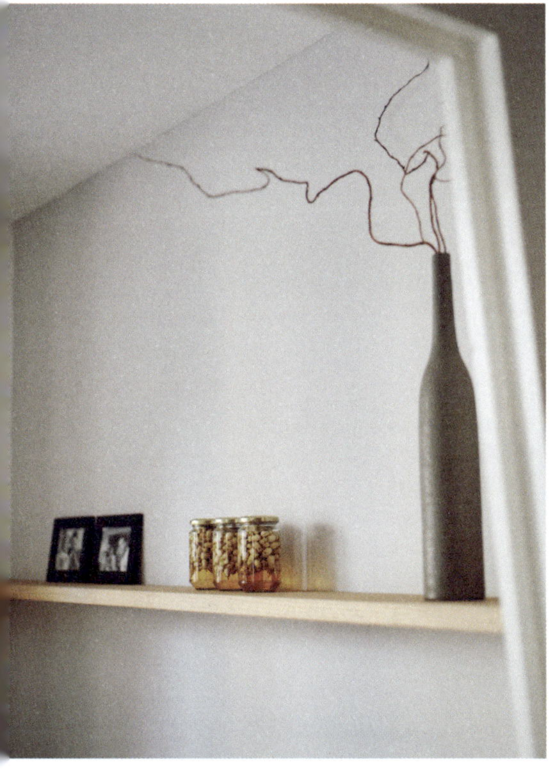

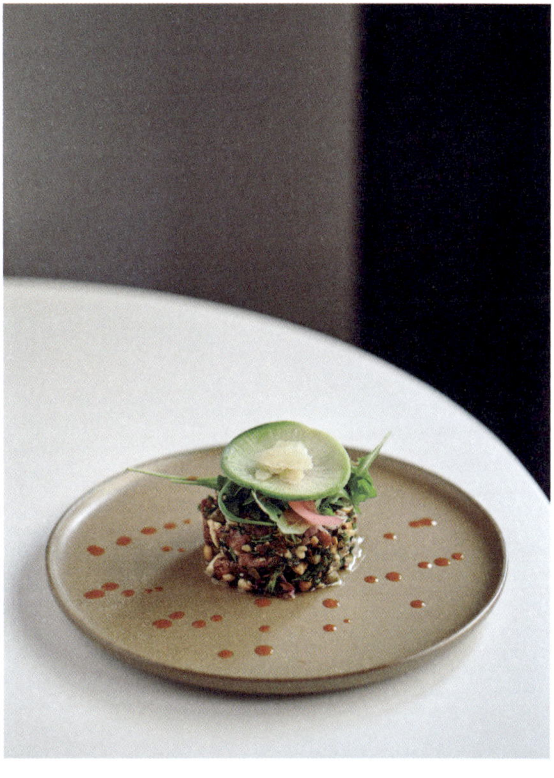

ATELIER DE CÉZANNE

Museum

9 avenue Paul Cézanne, 13090 Aix-en-Provence
+33 (0)4 42 21 06 53
cezanne-en-provence.com

The studio of Cézanne is small but enchanting. On the outskirts of Aix-en-Provence, the captivating atelier was the artist's workplace from 1902 to 1906 and it was here that he created some of his greatest works, including 'The Large Bathers'.

There is just one room to see, but the 'still lifes' arranged here include many of Cézanne's most recognisable motifs and relics. Spot the morbid skulls or the carefully arranged apples among the intriguing display. The beautifully kept furniture and artist's equipment evoke a very intense atmosphere for visitors. It seems fitting to visit the workplace of an artist who was inspired so much by the light and landscape of this area of Provence.

The studio hosts frequent cultural and gastronomic gatherings throughout the year.

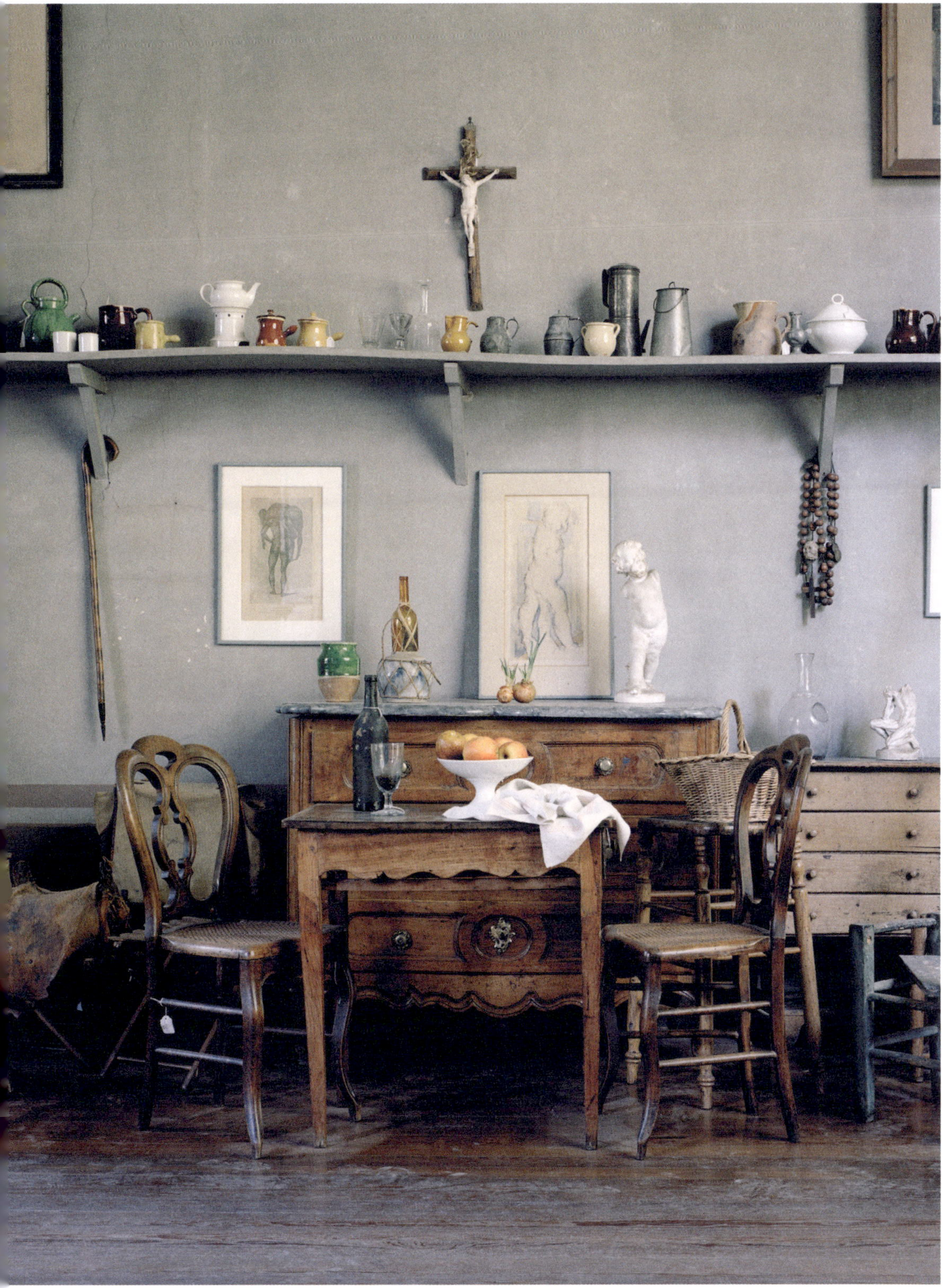

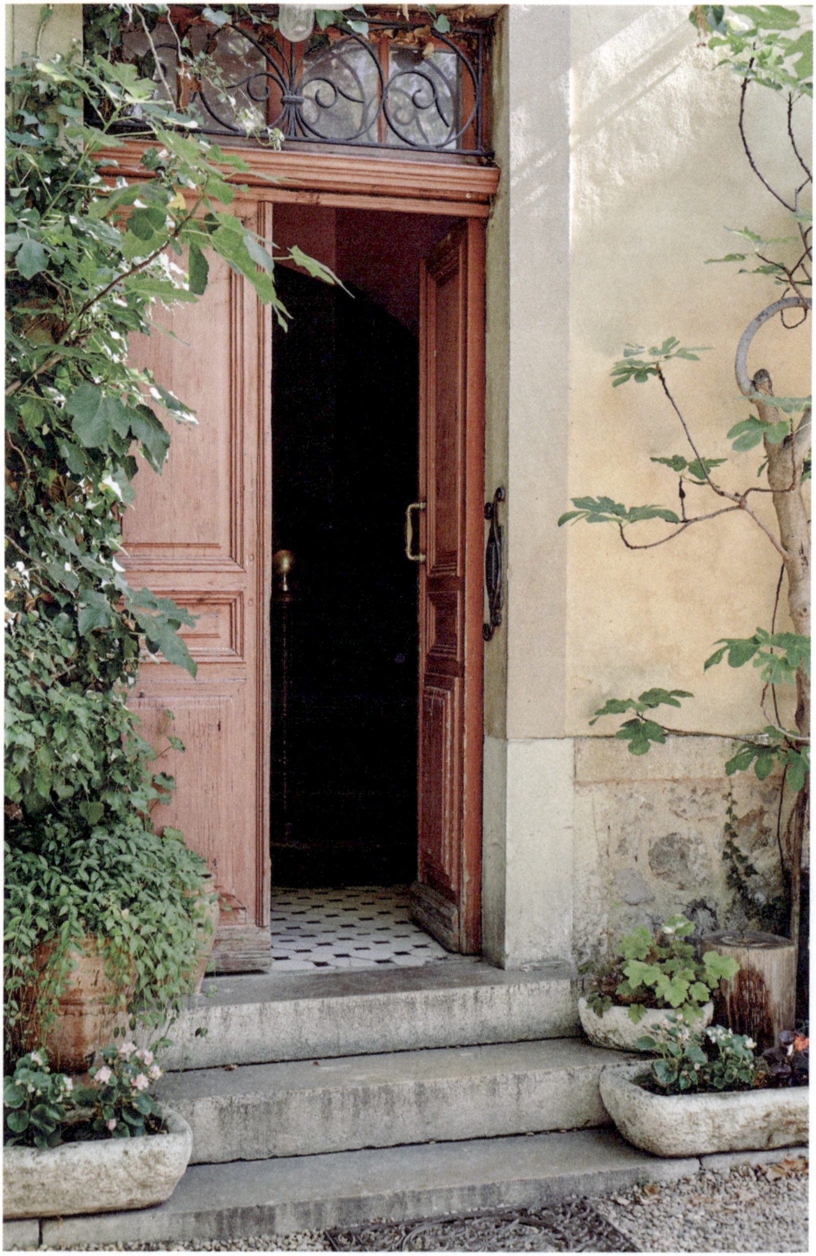

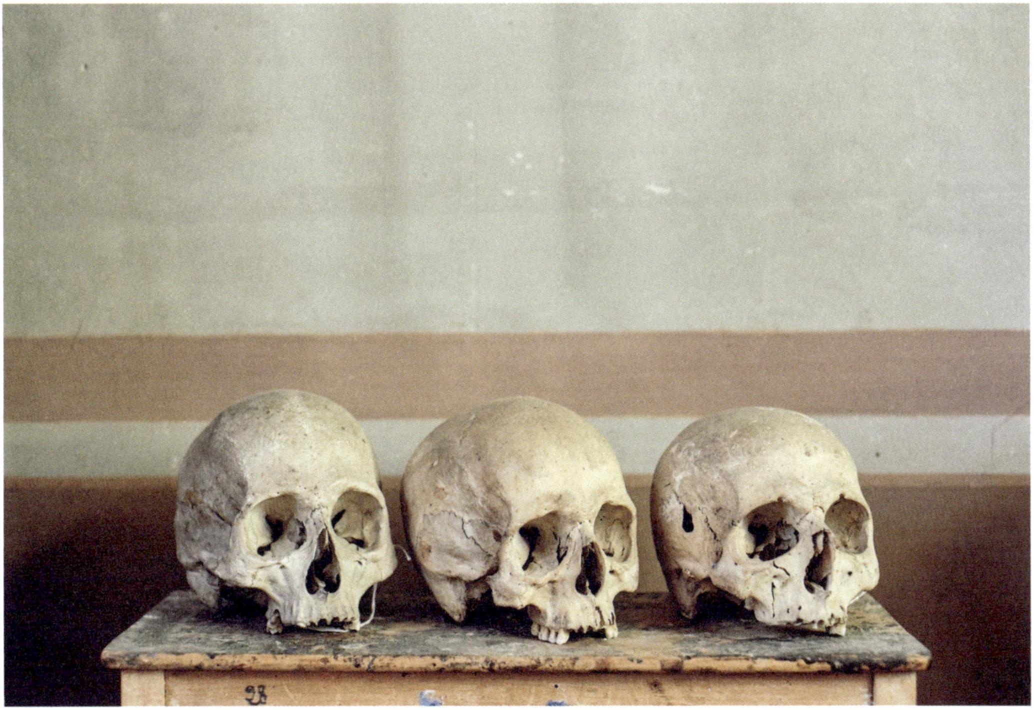

BASTIDE

Shop

14 rue Espariat, 13100 Aix-en-Provence
+33 (0)4 42 38 16 97
bastide.com

Frédéric Fekkai may be best known for celebrity hairdressing, but he has traded his flagship New York salon for a quieter life in Provence.

Aix-en-Provence is Fekkai's native home and where he has been busy growing the beautiful Bastide brand. With Bastide, he has captured the essence of this magical part of the world and transformed it into stylish but effective perfumes and skincare products. Bastide is very respectful of its authentic Provençal heritage; it is made by the very best local artisans and perfumers, using natural ingredients of the region.

Although the company does sell online, it is best to pick up your fragrant souvenirs at the sophisticated boutique in central Aix. Opt for a hand-blown 'Figue d'Ete' wax candle or a bottle of their 'Rose Olivier' Eau de Toilette.

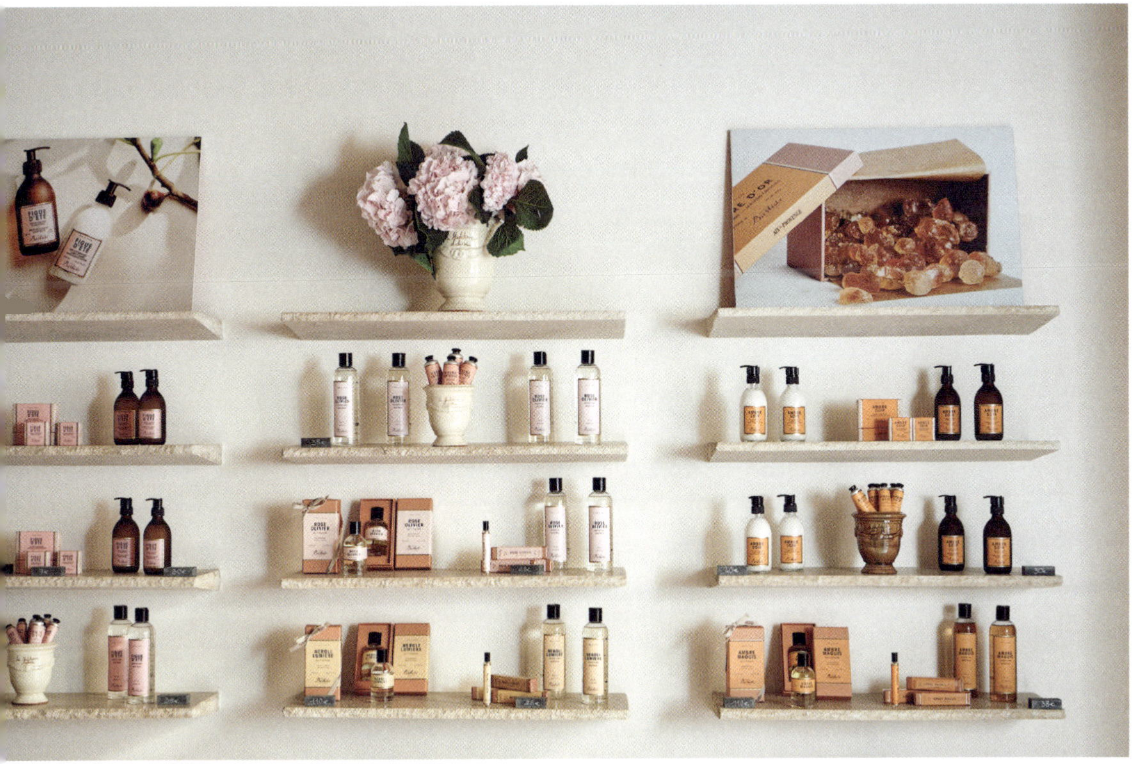

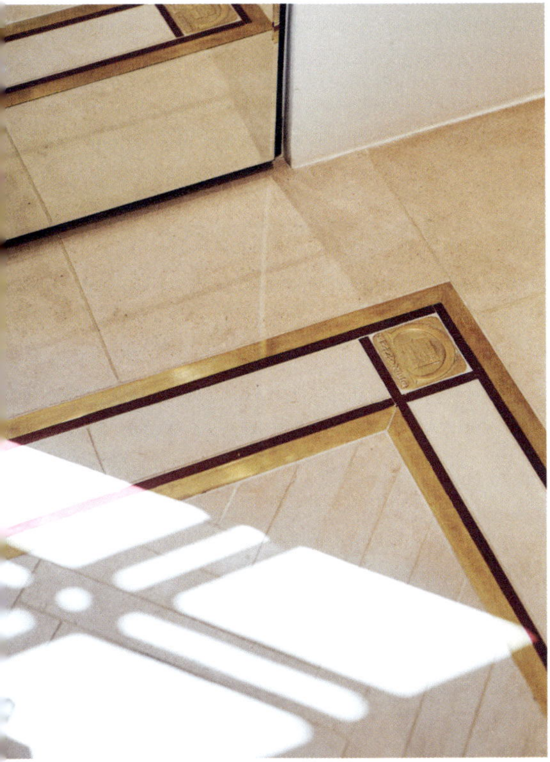

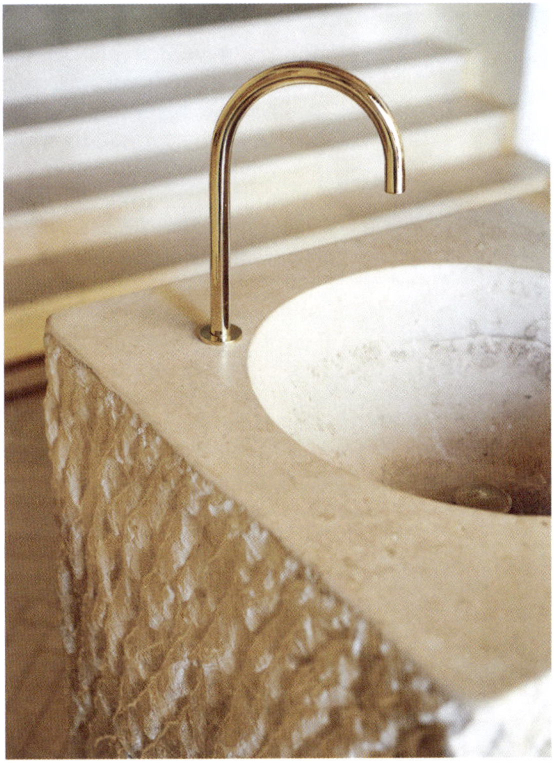

CHÂTEAU & VILLA LA COSTE

Cultural Domaine & Hotel

2750 route de la Cride, 13610 Le Puy Ste Réparade, near Aix-en-Provence
+33 (0)4 42 61 92 90
chateau-la-coste.com

Located in the wine region outside Aix-en-Provence, the La Coste estate is growing day by day and quickly becoming a creative culinary space unlike any other. Owner Patrick McKillen has transformed the 500-acre domaine to pay tribute to his favourite artists, chefs and designers.

The expansive vineyards and grounds feature works by some of the world's leading artists, including impressive sculptures by Louise Bourgeois, Tracey Emin and Richard Serra. Visitors can purchase a ticket to take a two-hour walk through the vines and olive groves to discover the wonderful art.

On the hilltop beyond the vineyards sits Villa La Coste, providing refined and luxurious accommodation. There are 28 Villa Suites here, each the definition of understated sophistication, all white with grand marble bathrooms and many with private terraces and plunge pools.

The restaurants at La Coste showcase the skills of world-renowned chefs Gérald Passédat - who presents French fine dining - and Francis Mallmann - who serves expressive and bold meat and fish dishes.

A day out at La Coste has something to entertain and indulge everyone.

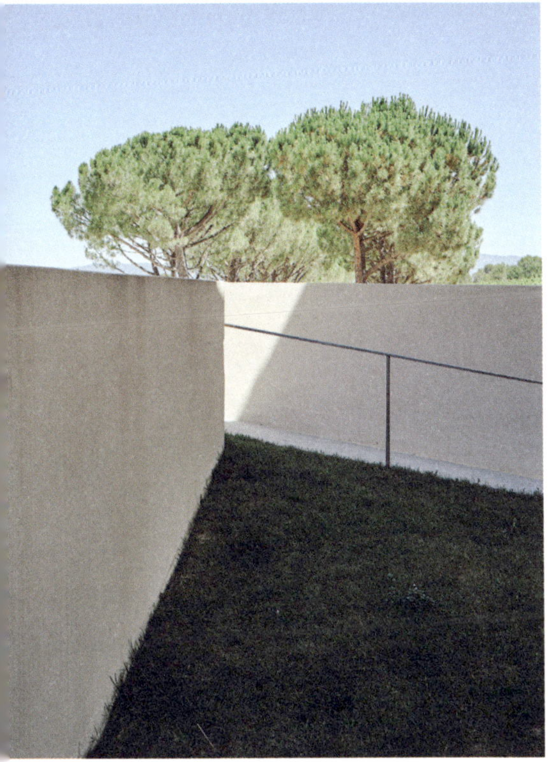
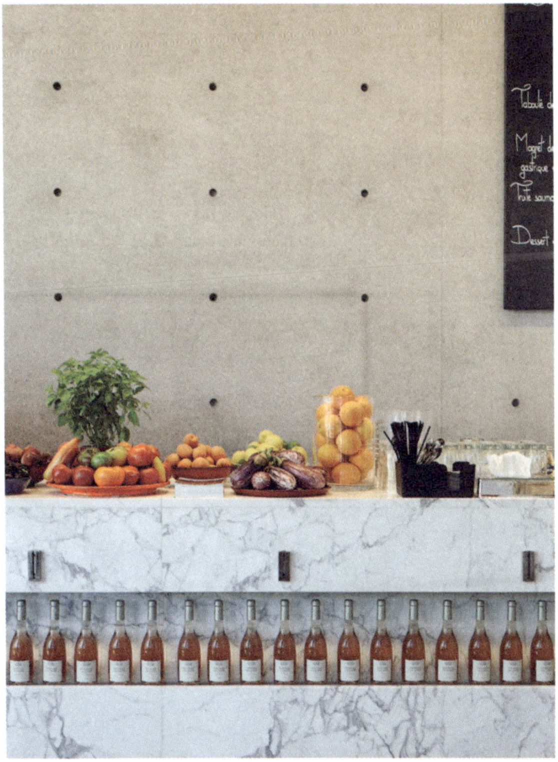
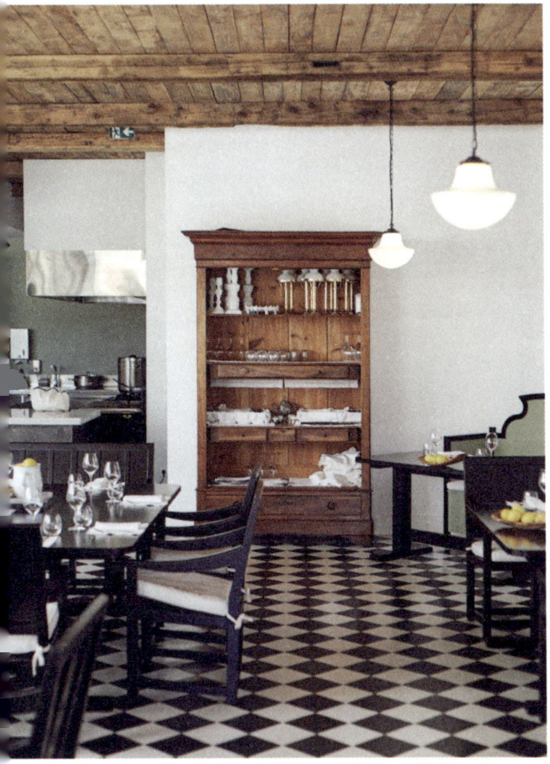
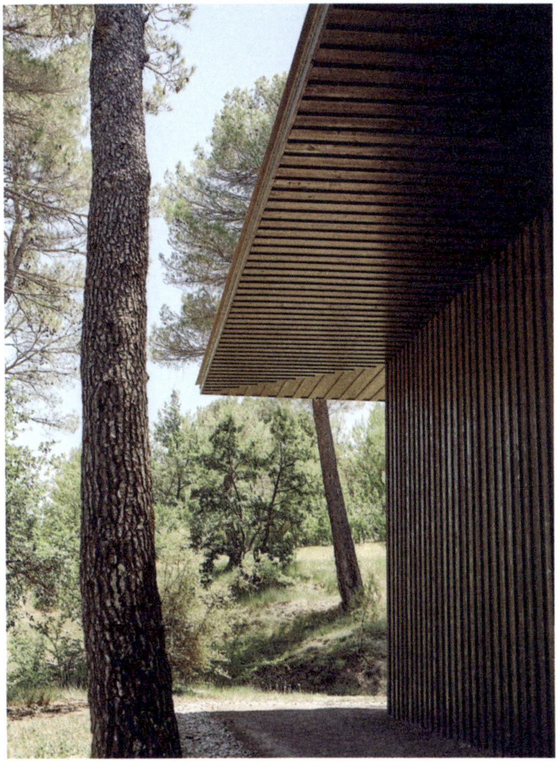

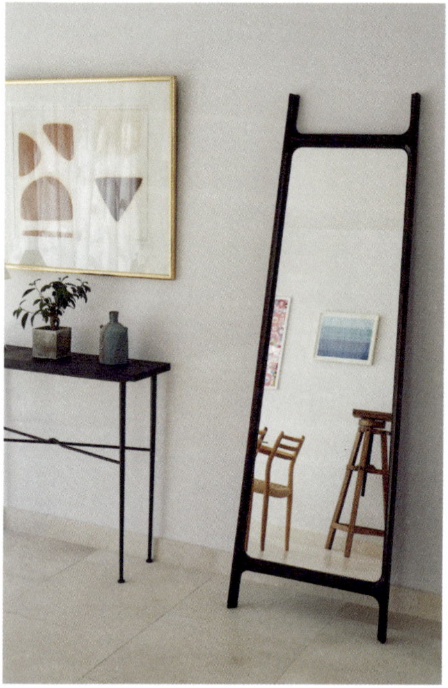
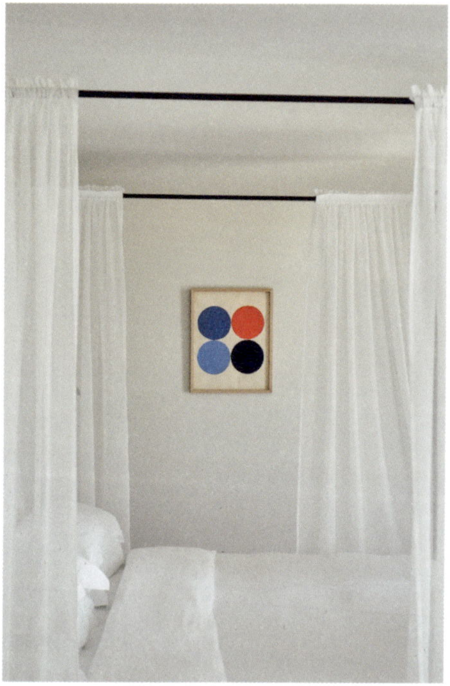
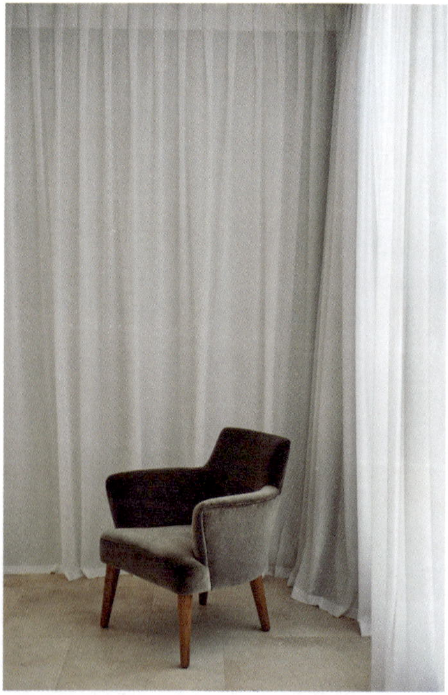
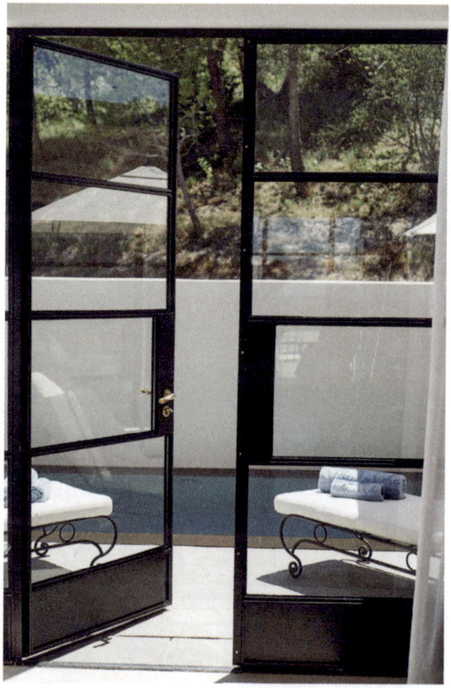

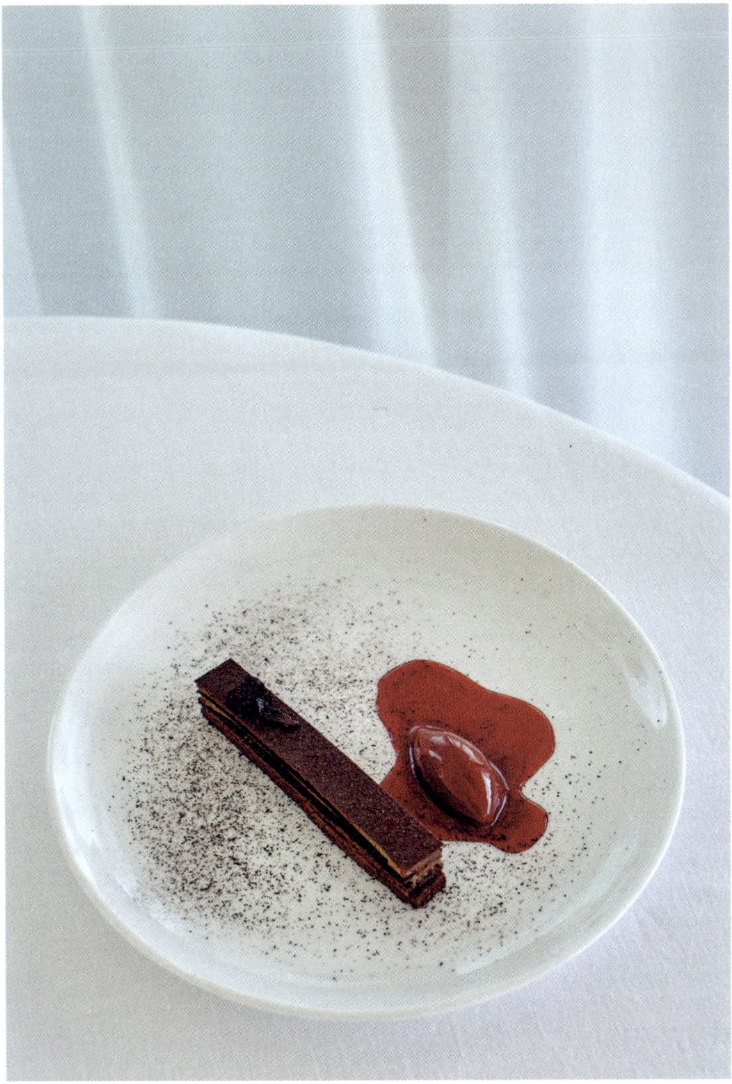

CHÂTEAU BARBEBELLE

—

Vineyard

D543, 13840 Rognes, near Aix-en-Provence
+ 33 (0)4 42 50 22 12
chateaubarbebelle.com

Nestled in the Aix-en-Provence countryside, Château Barbebelle is an idyllic house and vineyard, where wine has been produced since Roman times. The land has passed through four generations of the same family, which gives the property and wine a strong identity.

The 106-acre vineyard produces a variety of wines, of which the majority is on-trend rosé. Perhaps their best known wine is the Madeleine rosé, named after one of the owners of the estate. The wine is smooth and balanced, clean and crisp, a beautiful shade of pale peach. Château Barbebelle is very welcoming to visitors who wish to stop by for a little tasting session or to buy.

In summer, the château's central courtyard is used for cultural soirées and events.

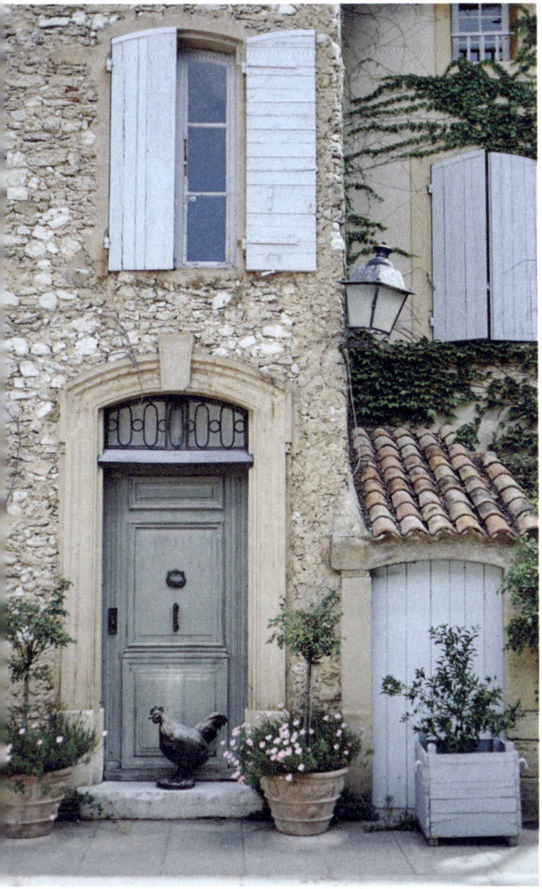
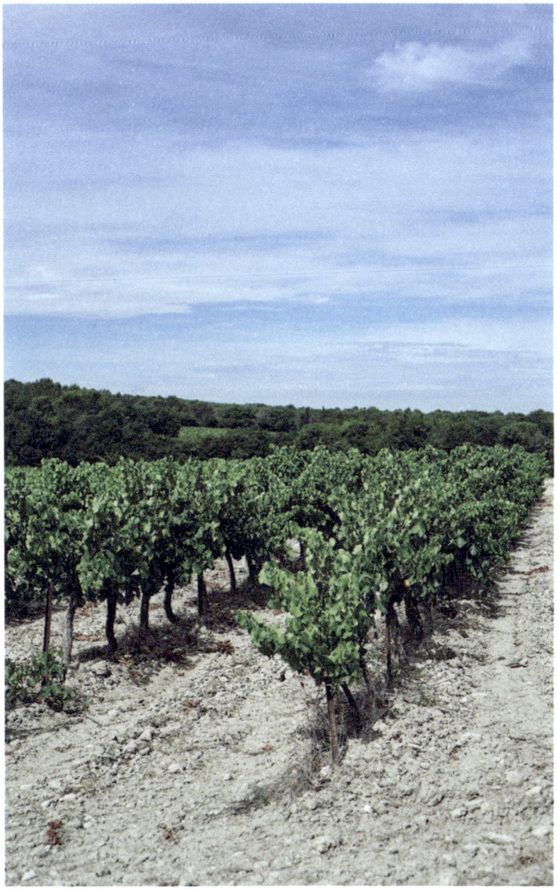
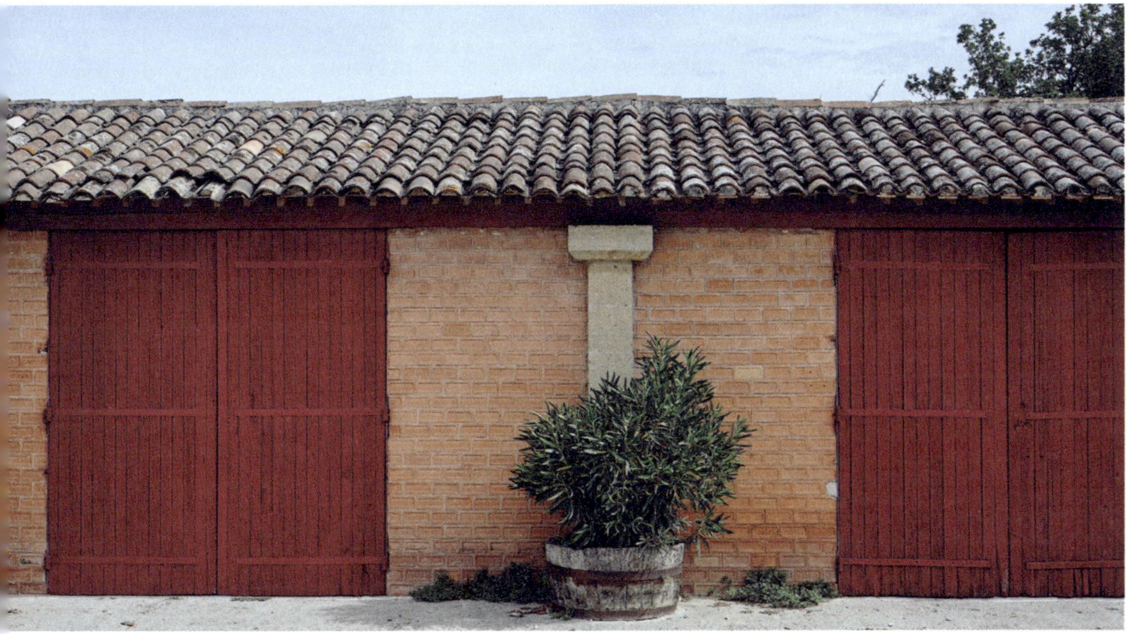

LA BASTIDE DE GORDES

Hotel

Rue de la Combe, 84220 Gordes, Luberon
+33 (0)4 90 72 12 12
bastide-de-gordes.com

Gordes is one of the most iconic and picturesque villages in Provence, perched on a slope in the heart of the Luberon.

The prestigious and ornate hotel, La Bastide de Gordes is found in the centre of the village. The spectacular building sits on 12th century ramparts and extends back into the rock. Jaw-dropping panoramic views are visible from most floors. The 40 bedrooms are each uniquely designed; a careful mix of antique artworks and historic furniture combined with modern amenities.

The hotel's sparkling Sisley spa is a calm and luxurious retreat for patrons and visitors. Guests can revitalise in the hot and cold sensory showers, book in for an al fresco treatment or soak up the sun at the outdoor pool.

On Sundays, the hotel's brunch at L'Orangerie is a real treat, and dinner at La Citadelle is equally popular in either the opulent dining room or on the terrace under the stars. Gastronomic fans should not miss Restaurant Pèir by Pierre Gagnaire, where this master chef recreates typical French recipes employing old cooking methods and the latest inventive techniques.

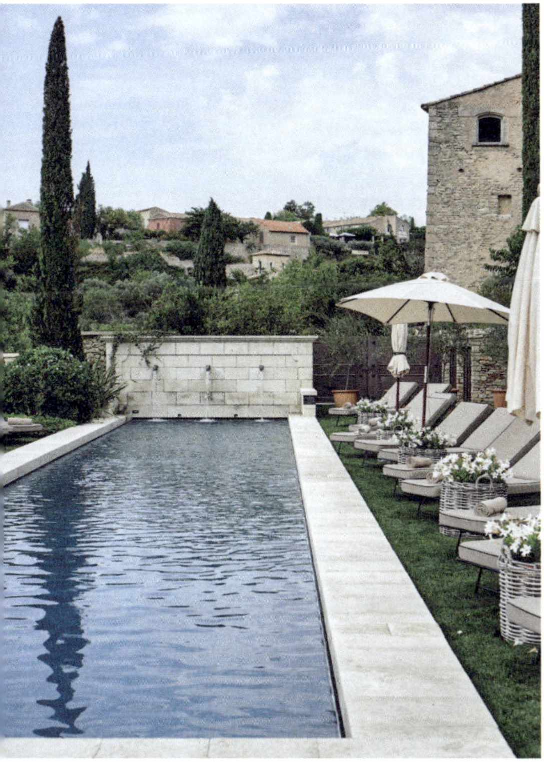
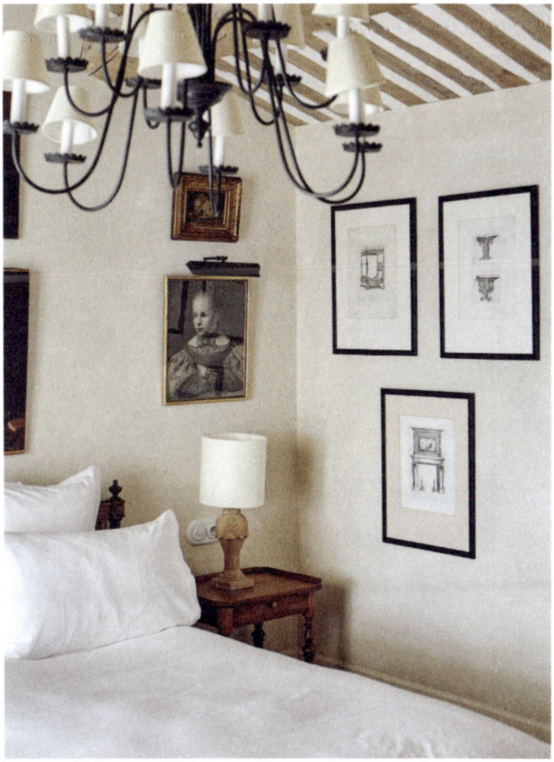
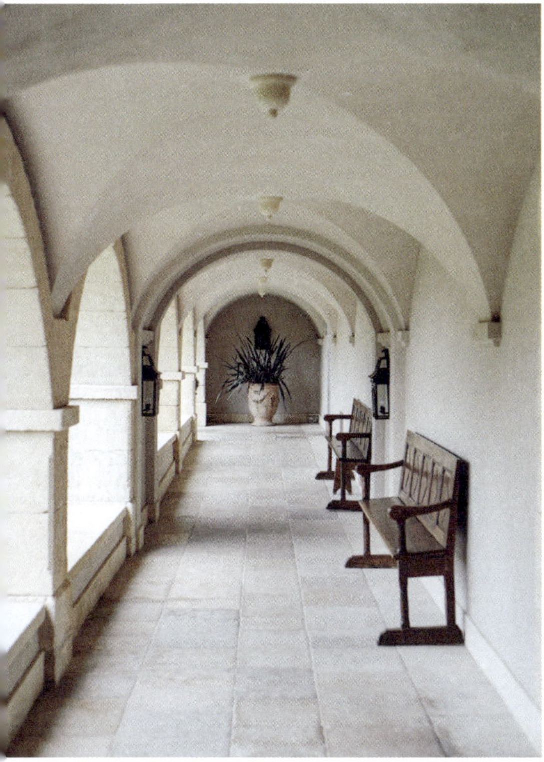
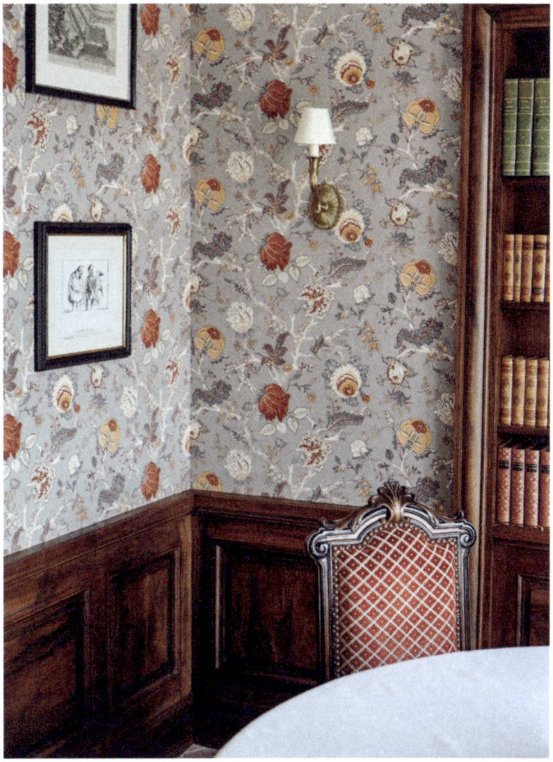

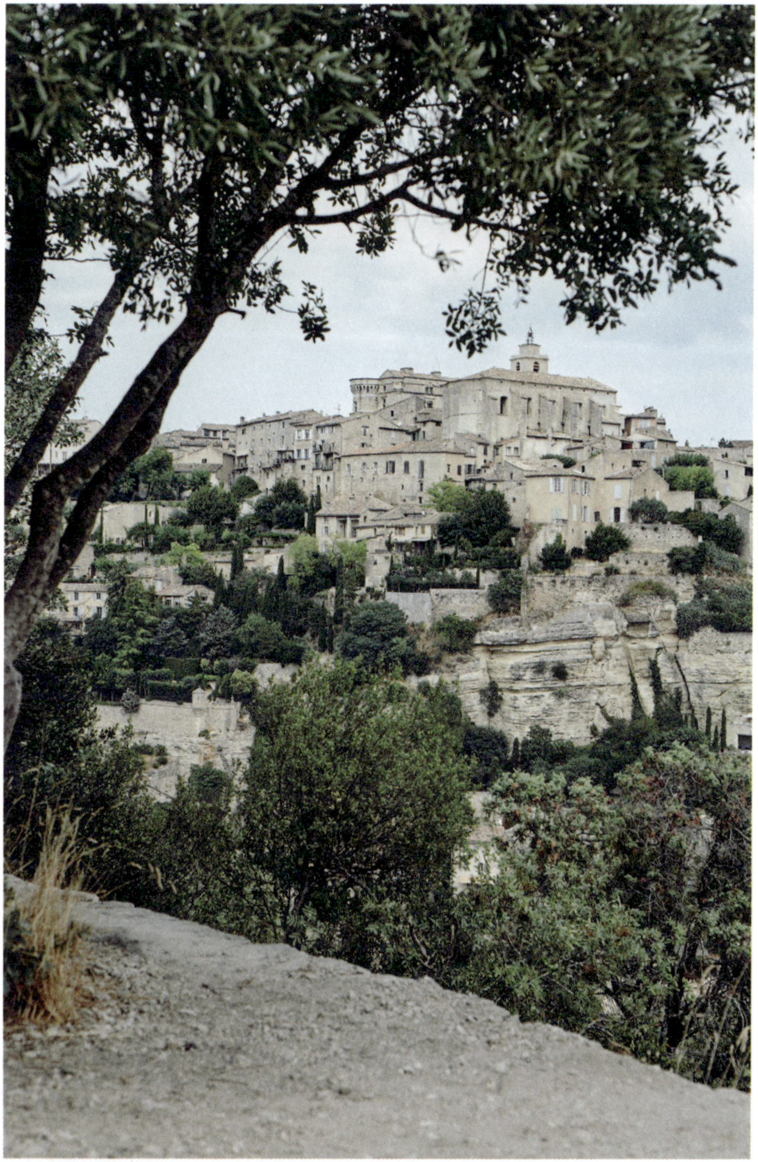

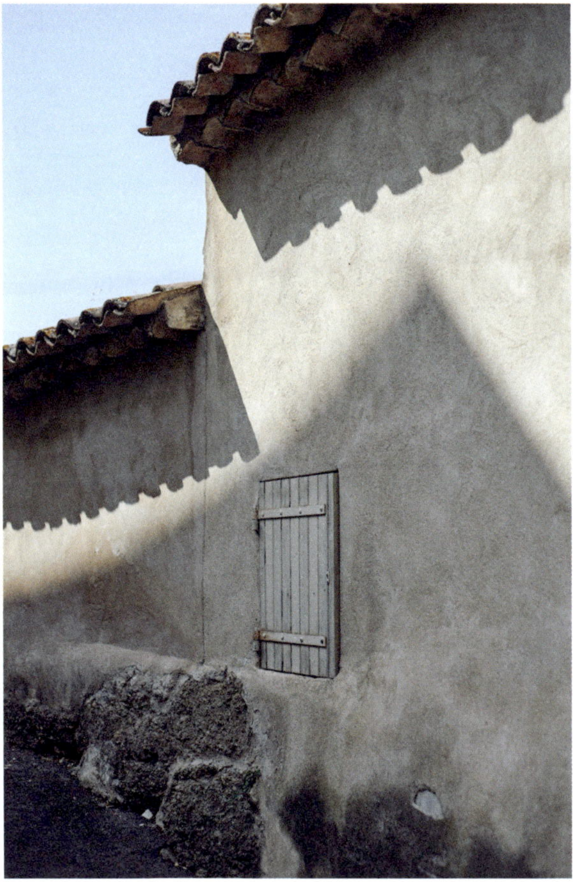

SCARAMOUCHE

Ice-cream Parlour

Cours Aristide Briand, 04280 Céreste, Luberon
+33 (0)4 92 79 48 82
glaces-scaramouche.com

Ice-cream lover or not, it is worth making a pilgrimage to Céreste in the Luberon to visit Provence's best artisan glacier.

New Yorker, Elizabeth Bard, and her Parisian husband, Gwendal Auffret, set up this charming ice-cream bar after settling in Provence. Located in a lovingly restored historic cellar on a quaint street corner in Céreste, the gelateria opened in 2013 and has grown in reputation ever since. Elizabeth also documented the story of Scaramouche in her popular memoir with recipes, Picnic in Provence.

This passion project has turned into a full-time family business and the couple work hard to showcase as many of the local ingredients and delicacies as possible, offering deliciously inventive and adventurous ice-cream flavours such as Provençal Saffron, Organic Lavender, Honey & Thyme, and sensational sorbets including Raspberry and Dark Chocolate. 1001 Nights is perhaps the most memorable flavour, the peppery spices of Raz El Hanout are combined with flaked grilled almonds, a nod to Gwendal's North African heritage.

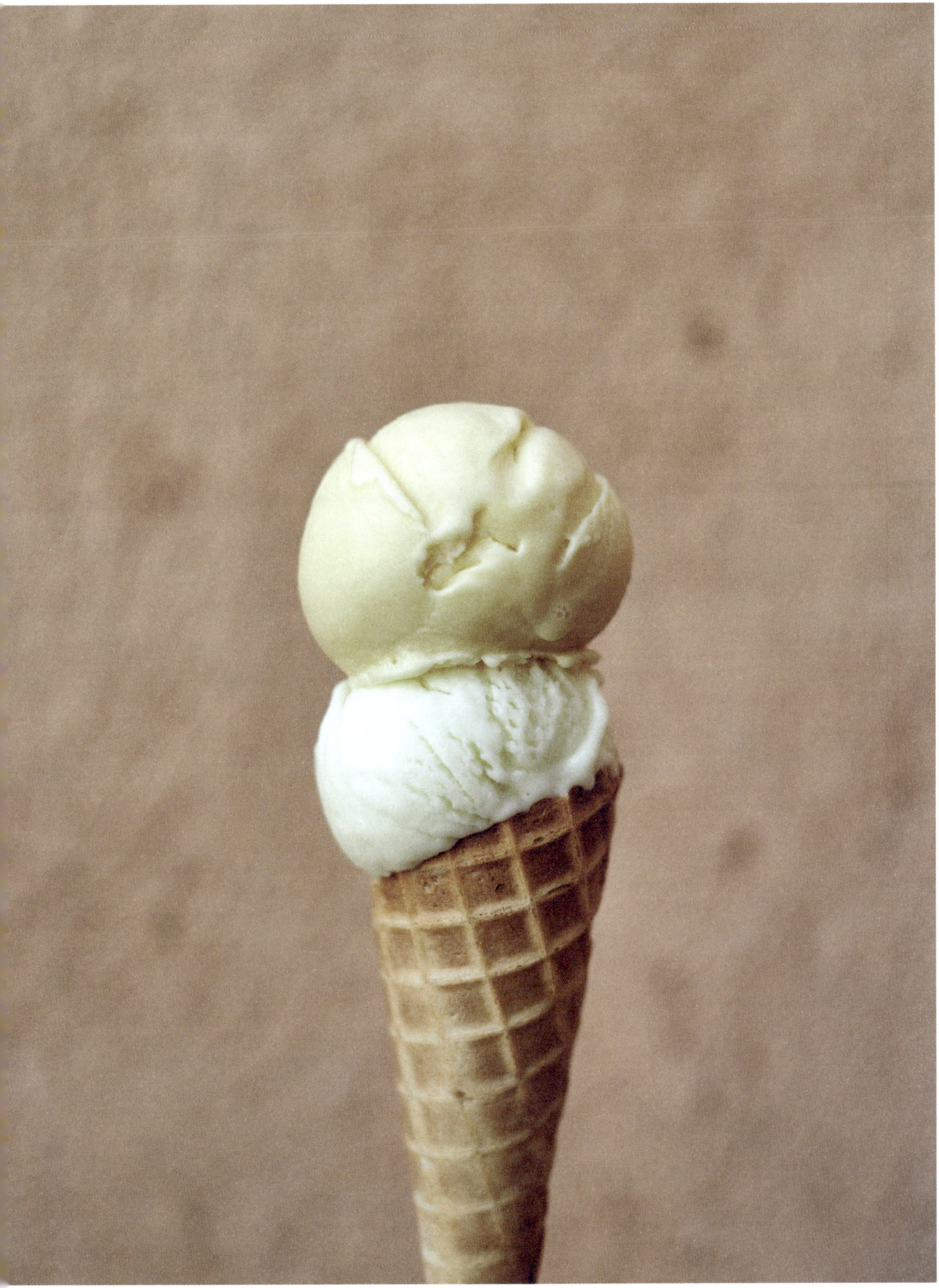

LA BASTIDE DE MOUSTIERS
—
Hotel & Restaurant

Chemin de Quinson, 04360 Moustiers-Sainte-Marie, Verdon
+33 (0)4 92 70 47 47
bastide-moustiers.com

La Bastide de Moustiers is found in the heart of Alpes-de-Haute-Provence. The house is remote and idyllic, surrounded by olive trees and lavender bushes.

Renowned chef Alain Ducasse discovered the bastide while exploring the area in 1994, and has transformed the quaint property into a luxury boutique hotel and destination restaurant. The eleven rooms and two suites are found among the gardens of abundant herbs, flowers and vegetables. The bedrooms have a rustic elegance and an authentic South of France charm with four-poster beds, soft natural linens and homely décor.

Chef Frédéric Garnier presents a short but refined menu of creative regional dishes. His cuisine is respectful of the homegrown ingredients, creating food that is vibrant, delicious and memorable.

The hotel has a helipad on site, which makes it the perfect Provençal getaway from the busy towns on the coast.

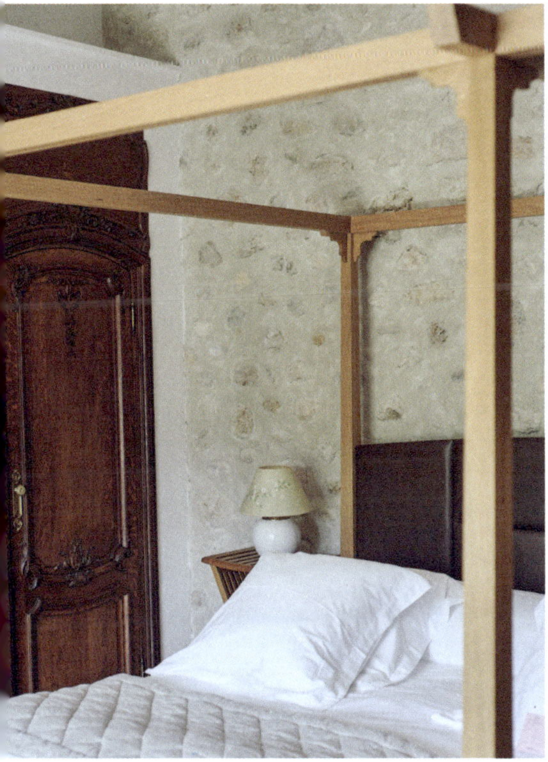
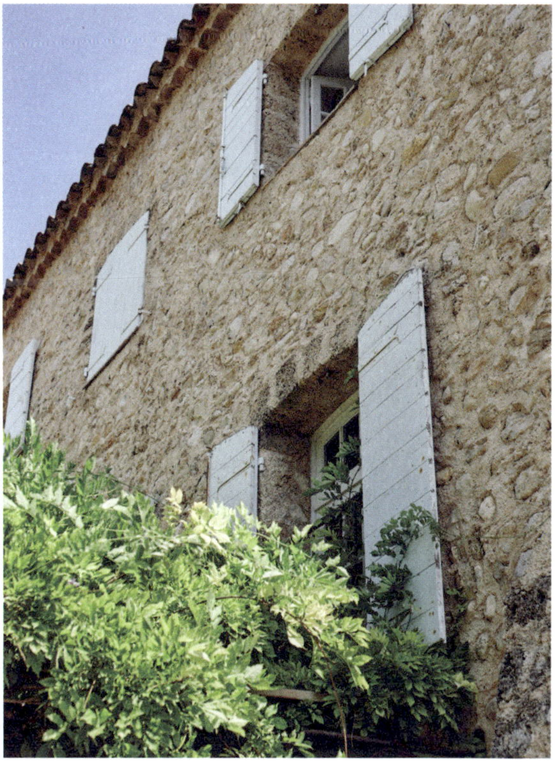
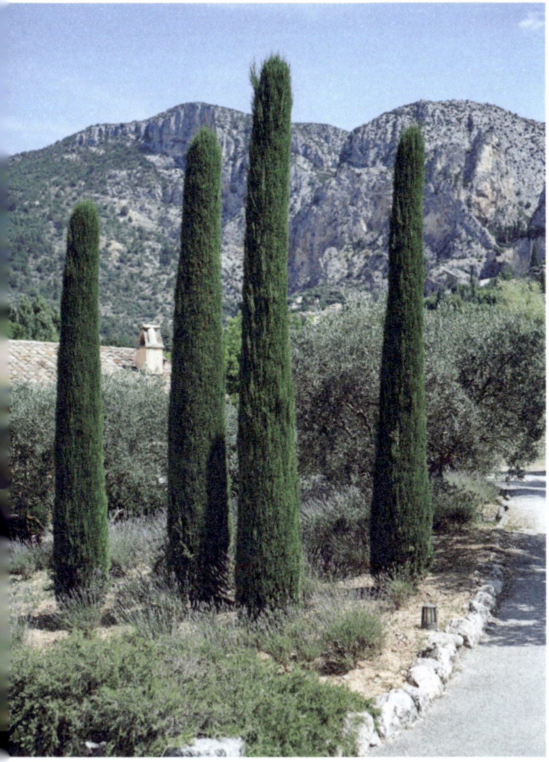
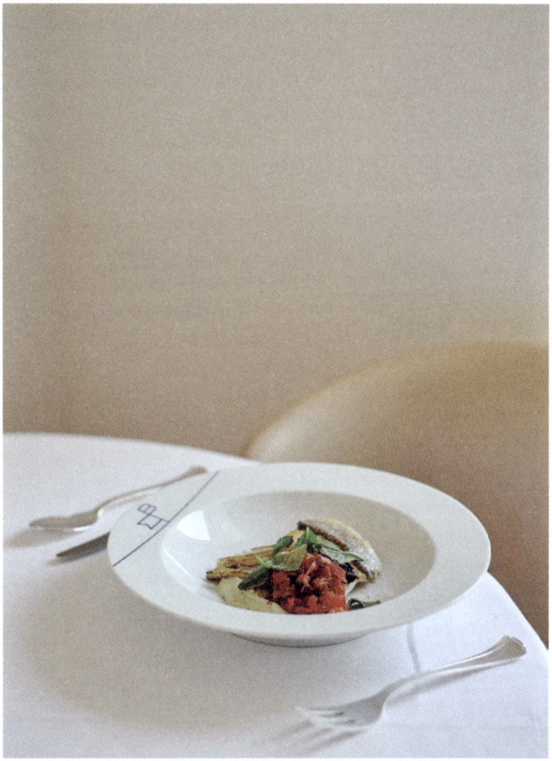

CHÂTEAU DE BERNE

Vineyard, Hotel, Restaurant & Cooking School

Route de Salernes, 83510 Lorgues, near Draguignan
+33 (0)4 94 60 43 60
chateauberne.com

Hidden away in the depths of the Provençal wilderness among 500 hectares of unspoilt countryside, Château de Berne deserves a visit for many reasons.

The house has been making wine for three centuries, but now also operates as a luxurious five-star hotel with a lavish spa, fine dining restaurant and distinguished cooking school.

For those visiting the area, the cooking school offers the opportunity to learn some valuable French culinary skills. Classes take place almost every day in the state of the art Provençal kitchen, with lessons focusing on topics such as Vegetables & Flowers from the Garden, French Classics, Spices and Petit Fours.

After a few hours in the kitchen learning the techniques and skills, you sit down and enjoy your creations. For a special occasion, Château de Berne's smart Michelin starred restaurant serves elaborate dishes by head chef Benjamin Collombat.

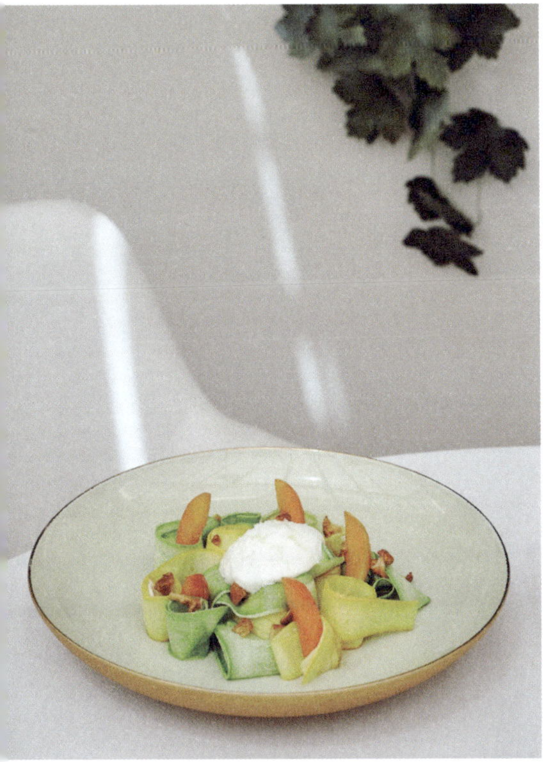
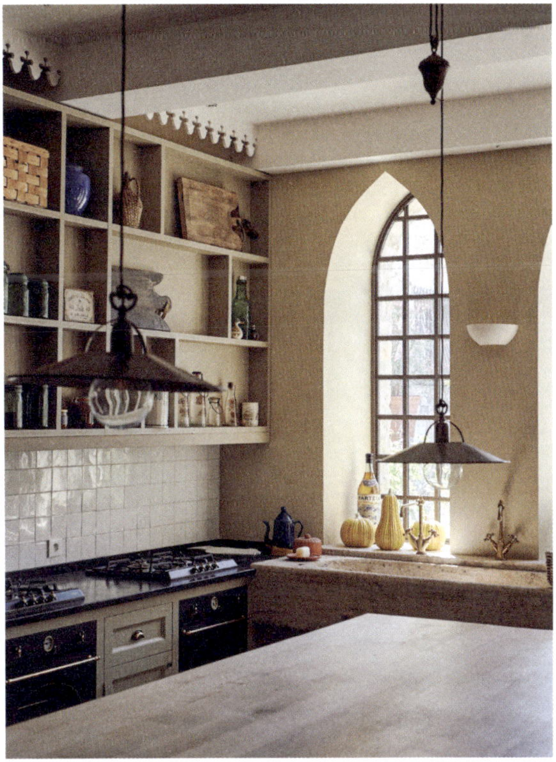
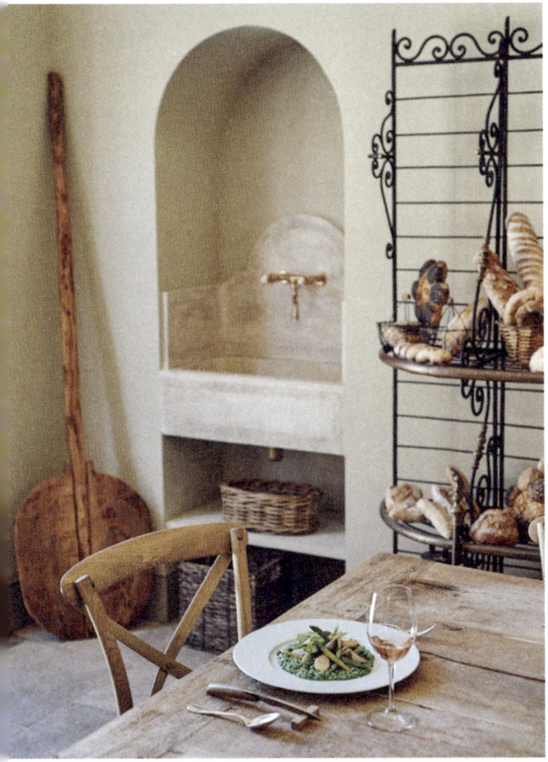
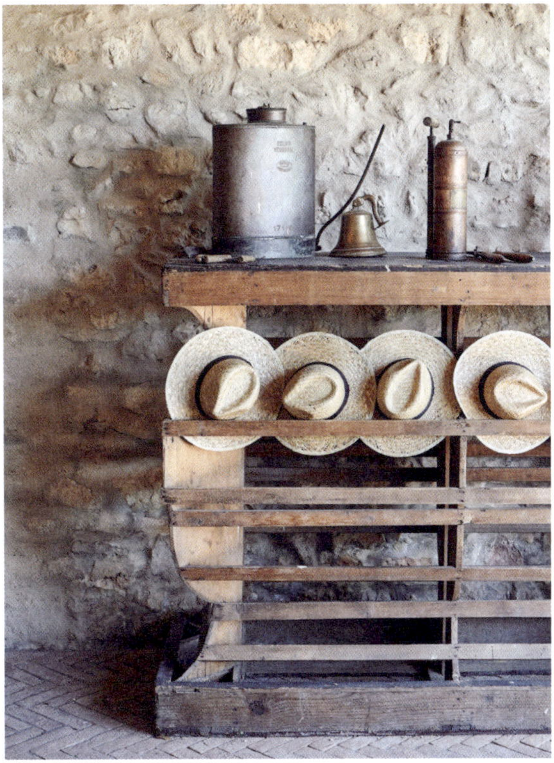

LE RELAIS DES MOINES

—

Restaurant

Route de Sainte Roseline, 83460 Les Arcs-sur-Argens, near Draguignan
+33 (0)4 94 47 40 93
lerelaisdesmoines.com

It is not difficult to find fine dining establishments in Provence, but very few have the understated charm of Le Relais des Moines. Perched on a hill outside Les Arcs, this Michelin starred restaurant is an authentic destination for a long lazy lunch.

Husband and wife team Géraldine and Sébastien Sanjou manage the restaurant and the kitchen respectively. They are a dynamic duo who complement each other to provide top service and gastronomic cuisine in a friendly and atmospheric restaurant. In summertime, the terrace has a breezy warmth, sheltered by a leafy canopy. Chilled local rosé is served and seasonal ingredients take centre stage. Inside, the restored 16th century house provides a cosy and romantic setting for evening meals.

The menus change regularly dependent on the produce Sébastien can source from local farmers. Opt for the reasonably-priced lunch menu while admiring the idyllic views over the Var and listening to the cicadas chirp in the background.

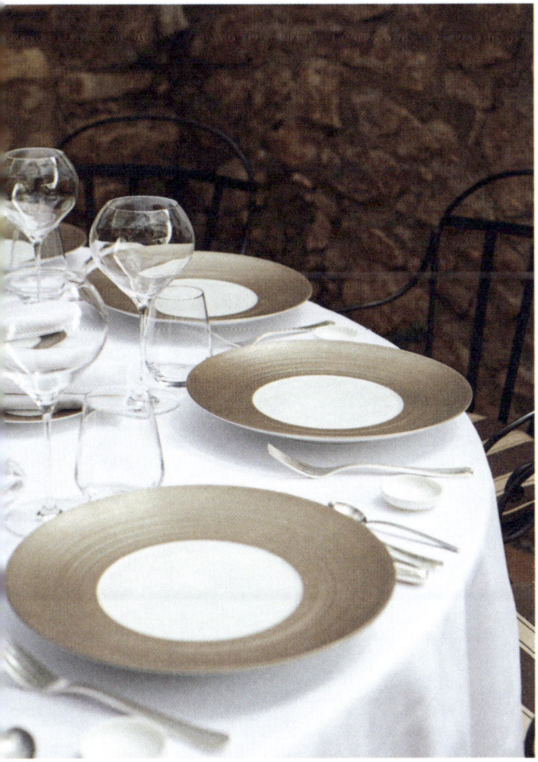
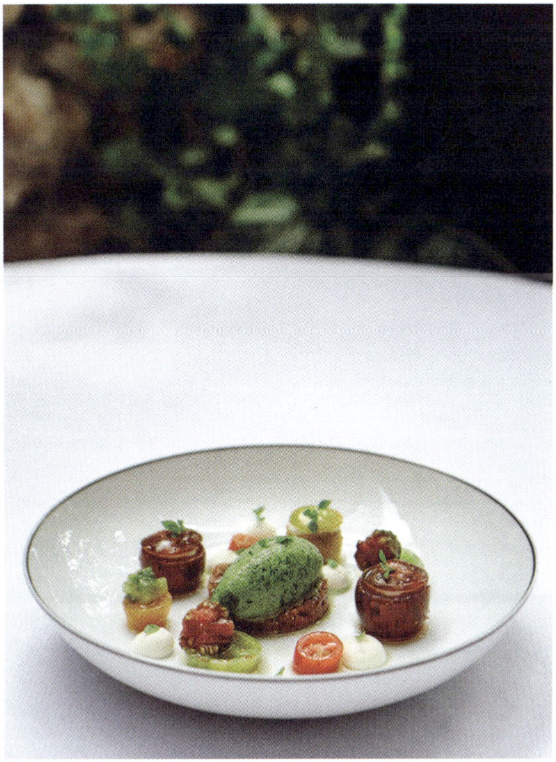
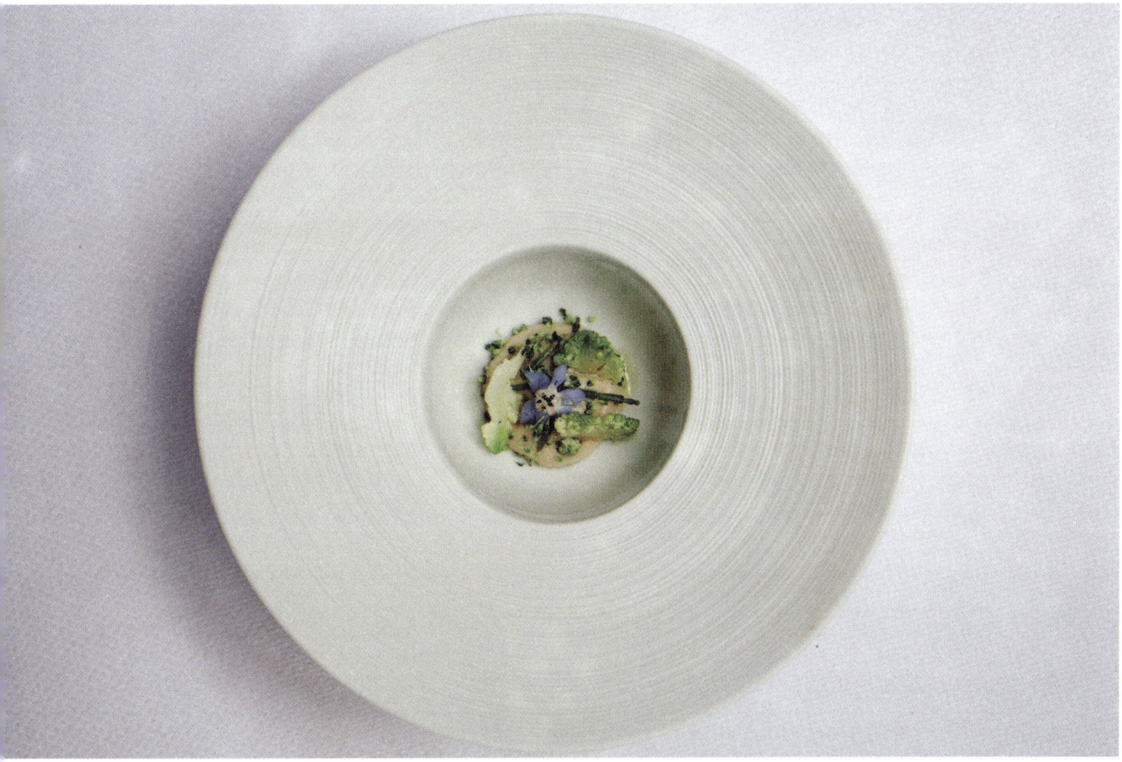

CHÂTEAU SAINTE-ROSELINE

Vineyard

Route de Sainte Roseline, 83460 Les Arcs-sur-Argens, near Draguignan
+33 (0)4 94 99 50 30
sainte-roseline.com

There are so many wonderful wineries to choose from when visiting this area of France. Château Sainte-Roseline's one thousand year terroir, 12th century cloisters and magical chapel make it one of the most special in the region.

After centuries of grape cultivation, it is hardly surprising that the fruit, which grows around Château Sainte-Roseline, makes such outstanding wine. From the 108 hectares, eleven grape varieties are grown, making award-winning red, white and rosé wine. Over half the production is for rosé, of which the Lampe de Méduse is the most expressive and popular.

Perhaps the most memorable part of the estate is the historical chapel where, since 1329, the body of Sainte Roseline has been preserved in a crystal glass case. Many great artists have celebrated this saint and her achievements (most famously the Miracle of the Roses) and Marc Chagall's remarkable mosaic, depicting the feast of the angels, is found in the chapel.

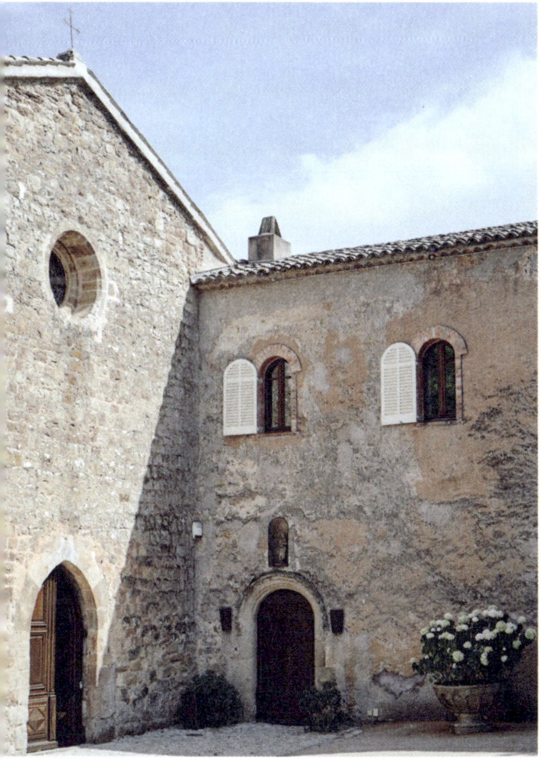
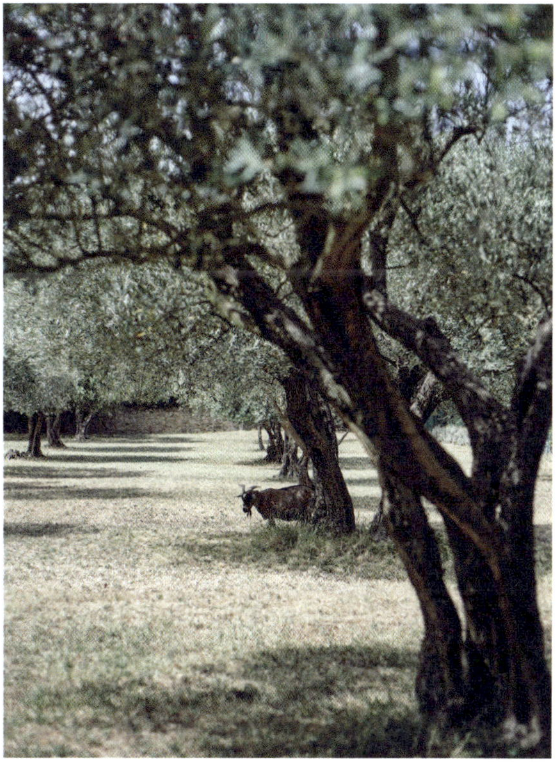
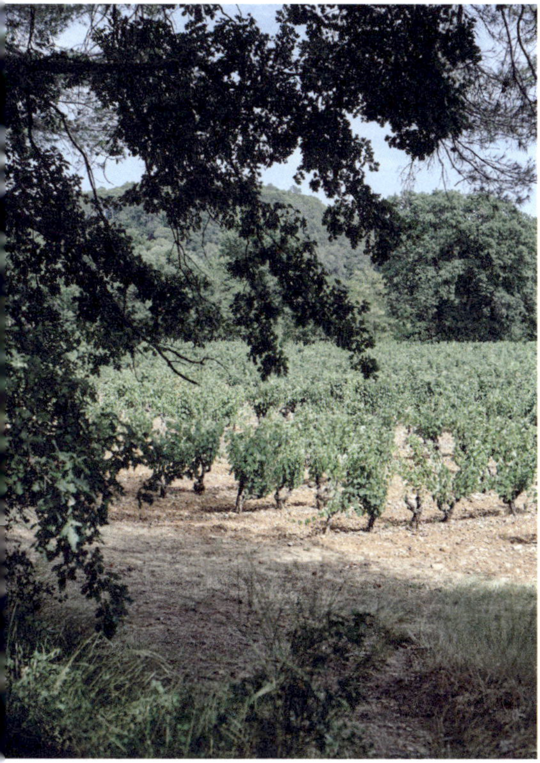
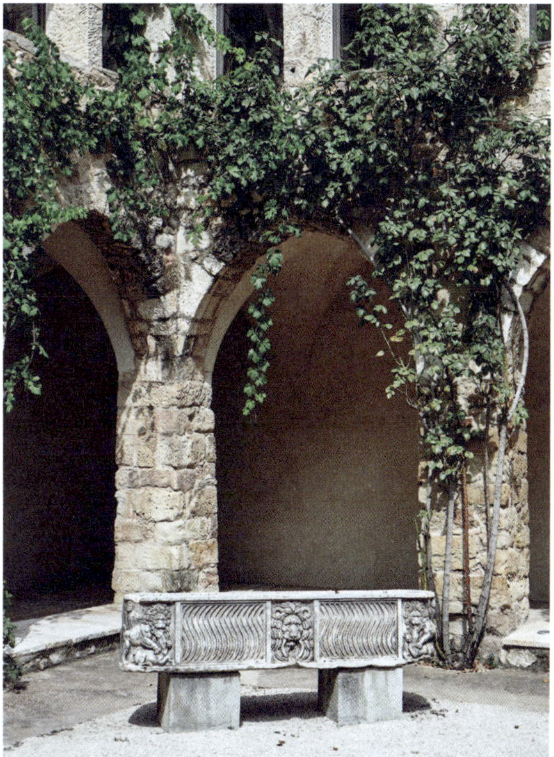

MUSÉE DE L'ANNONCIADE

Museum

Place Grammont Le Port, 83990 Saint-Tropez
+33 (0)4 94 17 84 10

Saint-Tropez is renowned for glitzy celebrity culture, but there is also a quiet and charming side to this historic town.

The Annonciade Museum is found near the main port and is an atmospheric 16th century chapel converted into a museum that houses an impressive collection of modern paintings and sculptures. The pale pink building, with its small leafy courtyard, has a fairy tale feel from the outside. Inside, the peaceful gallery is a contrast to the busy streets of Saint-Tropez. The white walls display colourful visions: Provençal scenes, seascapes and countryside views.

The two floors exhibit works dating from 1890-1950 by prominent artists who worked in Saint-Tropez at some point during their lives. Admire Fauve paintings by Matisse and Derain, and delicate Pointillist landscapes by Paul Signac who introduced many other artists to this part of the world.

MVSEE
DE
L'ANNONCIADE

PAN DEÏ PALAIS
—
Hotel

52 rue Gambetta, 83990 Saint-Tropez
+33 (0)4 94 17 71 71
pandei.com

Pan Deï Palais is an unusual taste of Indian majesty in Provence. This magnificent boutique hotel is discreetly located behind an unpretentious front door in the centre of Saint-Tropez's old town. Legend has it that Pan Deï Palais was built in 1830 as a token of love from a French General to a Punjabi princess (whose name was Bannu Pan Deï).

The modest entrance opens onto an elegant and warm palatial hallway, decorated in shades of red and gold, with characterful furniture and ornate artworks. The bedrooms are a fresh mix of pristine white walls, luxurious amenities and intricate details. There is a feel of sensuous luxury and cosy romance in every room. Downstairs, a turquoise pool is surrounded by lotus leaf patterned parasols and chic sunbeds, a calm sanctuary away from the buzz of town. The hotel's restaurant serves classic recipes with a twist, inspired by regional ingredients.

Pan Deï Palais is Saint-Tropez's best-kept secret, a rare taste of exoticism on the Riviera.

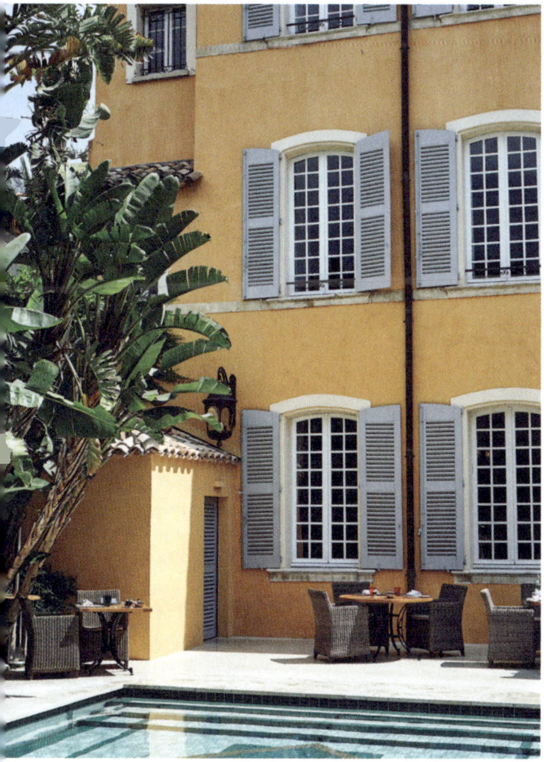
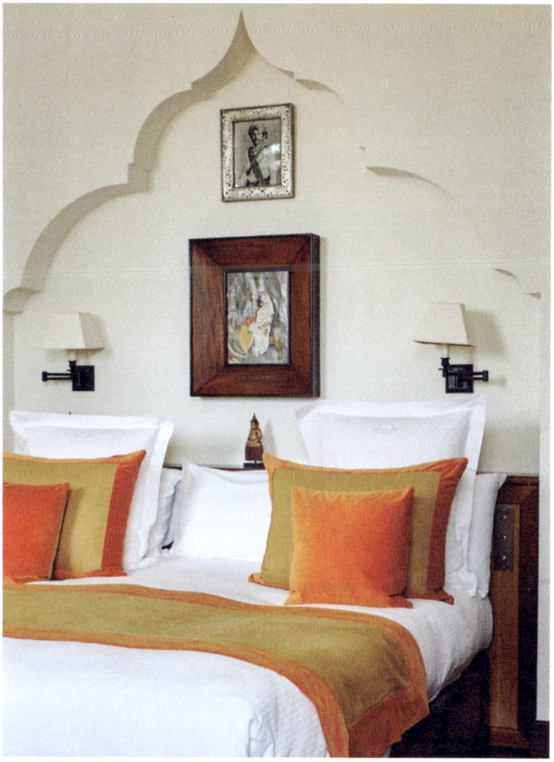
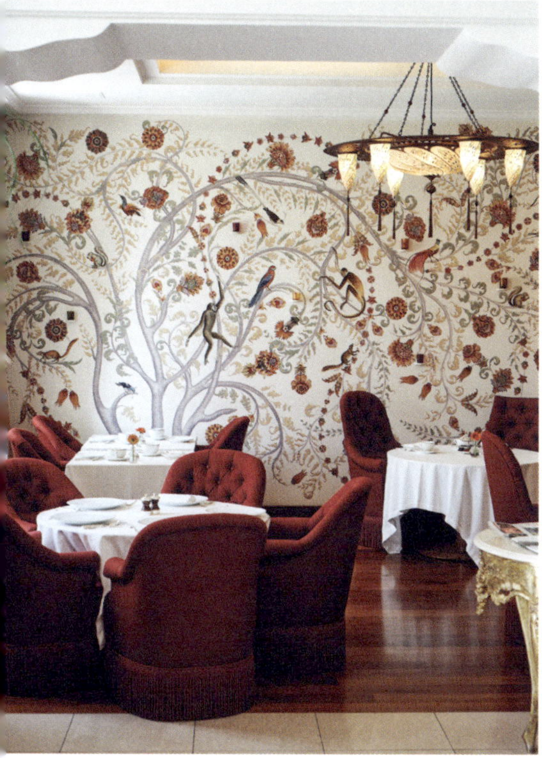
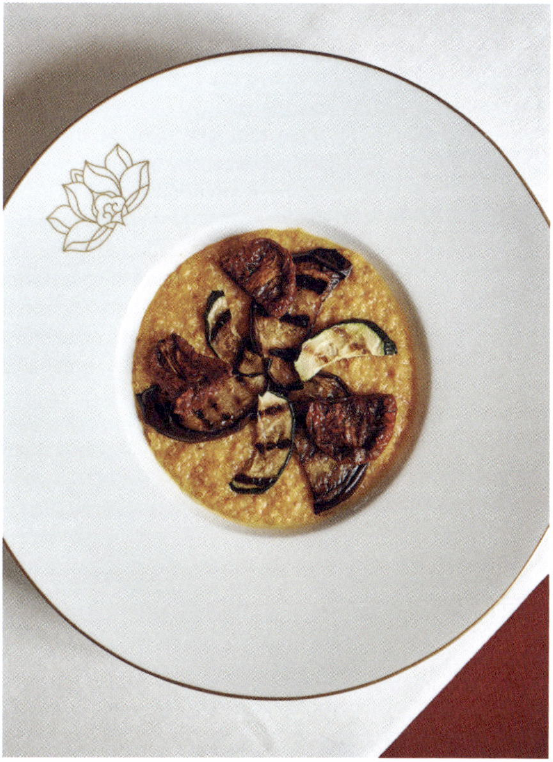

RONDINI, SANDALES TROPÉZIENNES
—
Shop

18-18Bis rue Georges Clemenceau, 83990 Saint-Tropez
+33 (0)4 94 97 19 55
rondini.fr

Saint-Tropez is crammed full of international designer brands, but if you hunt hard enough you can find a few special independent boutiques selling handmade crafts, designed and fabricated in town.

Rondini is perhaps the most popular artisan shop in Saint-Tropez. This family run business has been making legendary shoes for over 90 years and was the first sandal-maker in town. Dominique Rondini started the company in 1927, later joined by his son Serge, and recently his grandson Alain took the reins of the business. The design and materials have stayed largely the same for decades with sturdy French leather soles and bespoke attention to detail.

The tiny atelier is found down a busy backstreet in the centre of town. The shoes are made in a workshop at the back and then fitted carefully to your feet in the shop. The classic 'Tropéziennes' sandals are the most famous, with a unique and comfortable design, but there are many other styles to choose from to meet all your summer needs.

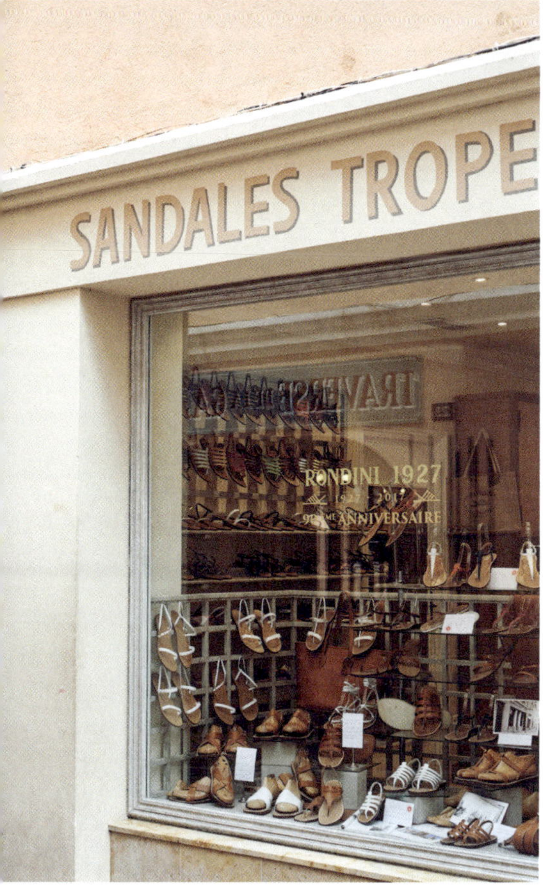
SANDALES TROPE
RONDINI 1927

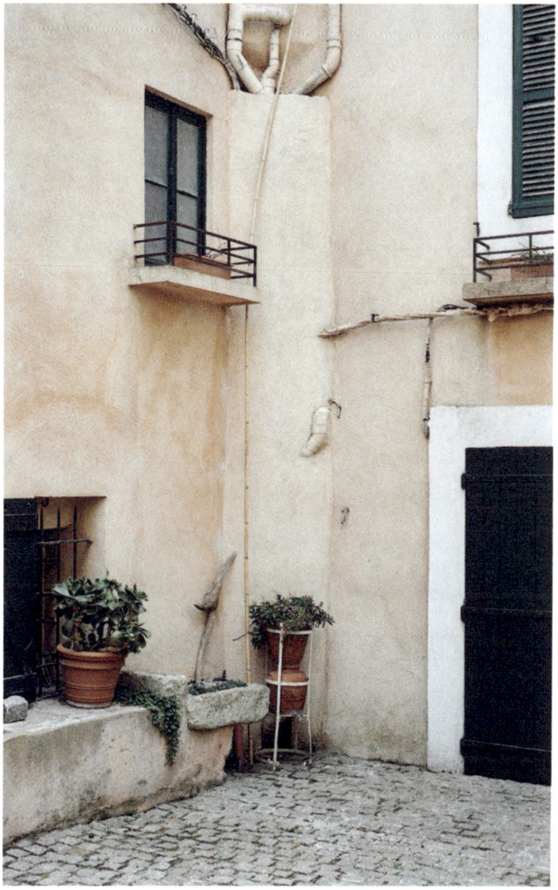

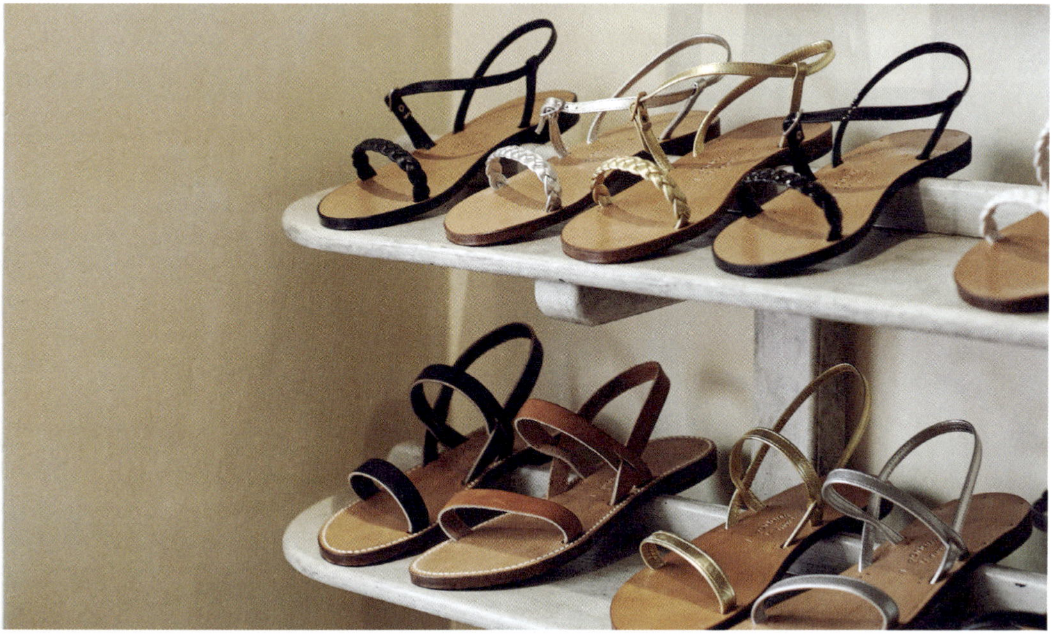

HÔTEL LES ROCHES ROUGES

Hotel

90 Boulevard de la 36e Division du Texas, 83530 Saint-Raphaël
+33 (0)4 79 33 01 04
hotellesrochesrouges.com

Les Roches Rouges is the first seaside property from Les Hôtels d'en Haut, a French hospitality group who own several properties in the Alps. This chic, stylish hotel has made its home in a stark white 1950s building on the coast just outside Saint-Raphaël.

The understated luxury and design-led interiors are unlike any other accommodation in the area, and the affordable prices mean the hotel is accessible for all style conscious travellers. The brilliant white bedrooms are sophisticated and fresh, with accents of natural beige and earthy orange. Architects Hugo Sauzey and Charlotte de Tonnac of Festen Architecture aimed to create a Riviera retreat with 'simple but noble materials' and every aspect feels very authentic from the polished concrete to the Céramiques du Beaujolais.

When it is time to eat, Les Roches Rouges has both a fine-dining option and a relaxed eatery serving Provençal specialities. Outside there are two swimming pools - one of which contains natural seawater - a pine tree shaded pétanque court, a cocktail bar, and deckchairs and loungers for soaking up the sun.

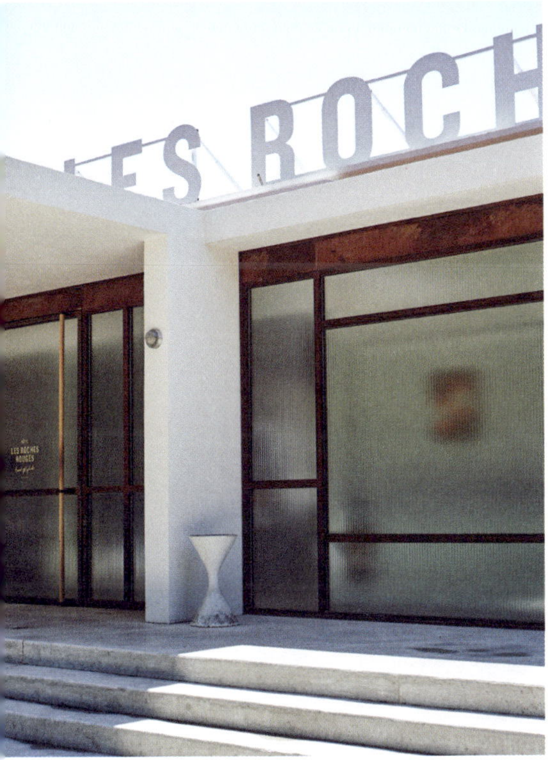
ES ROCH
LES ROCHES
ROUGES

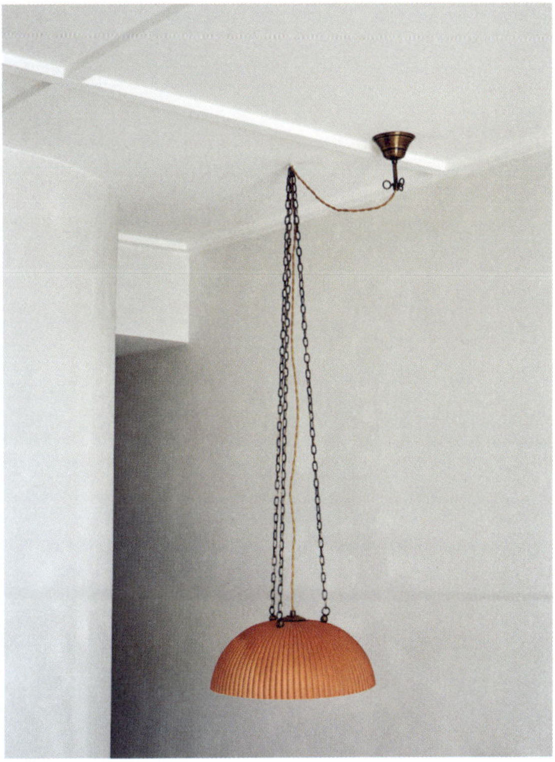

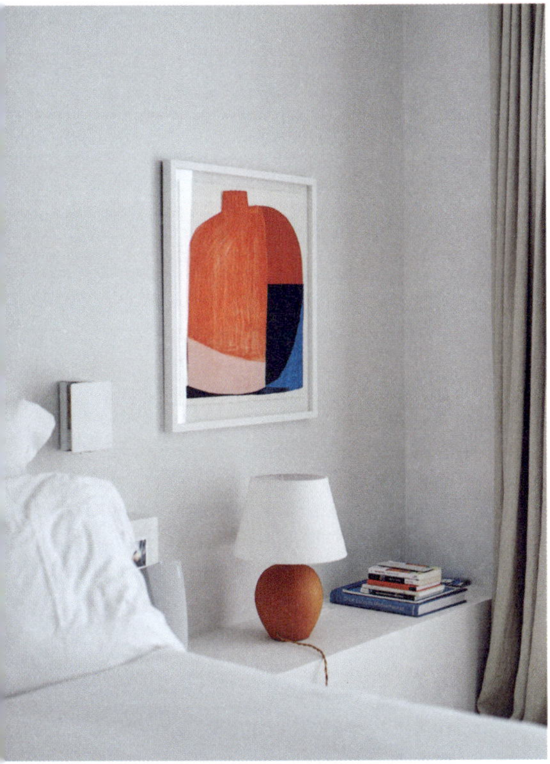

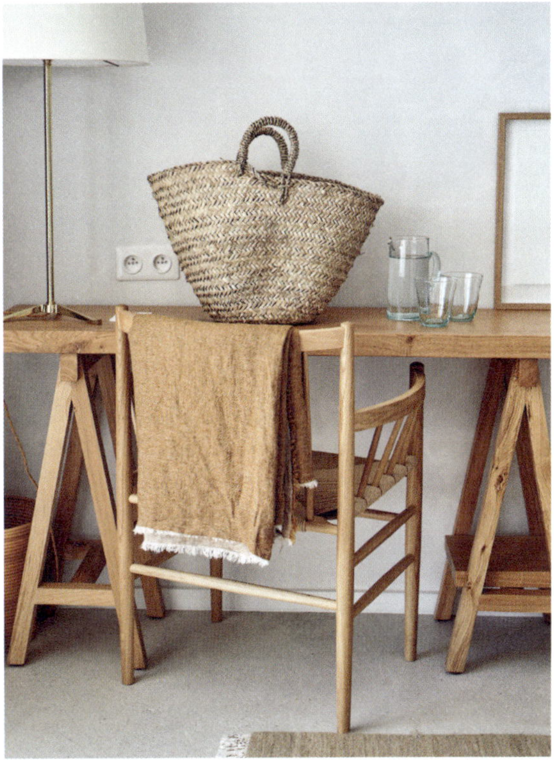

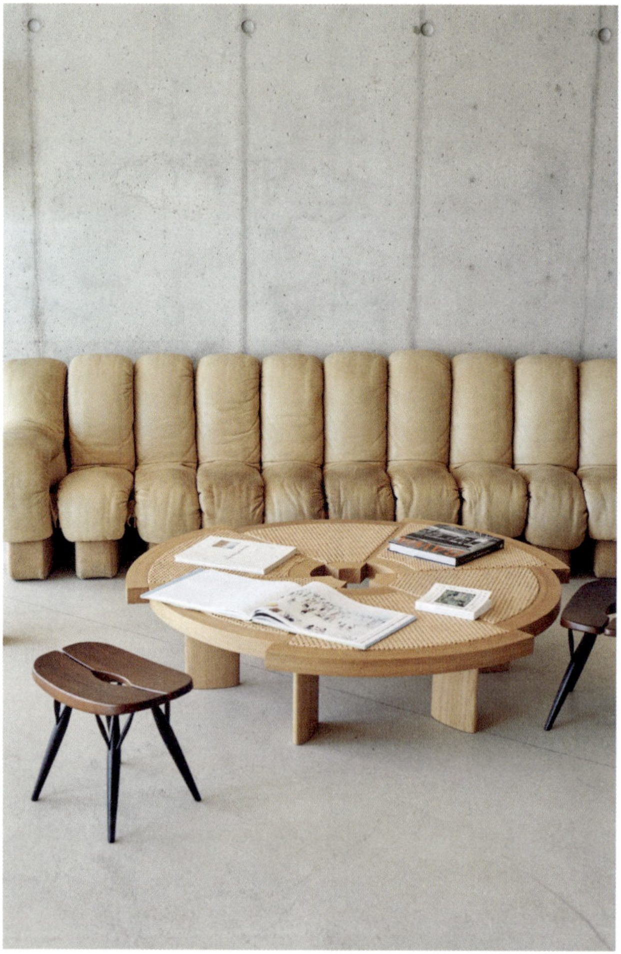

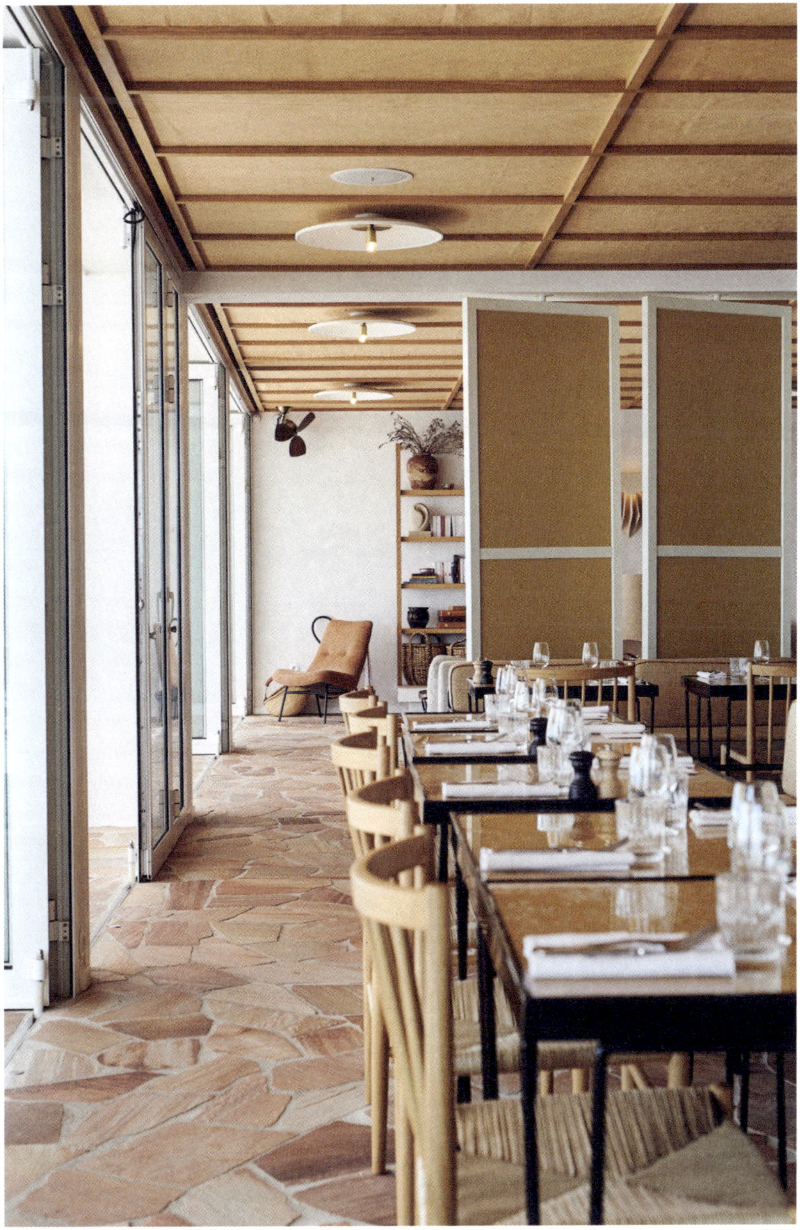

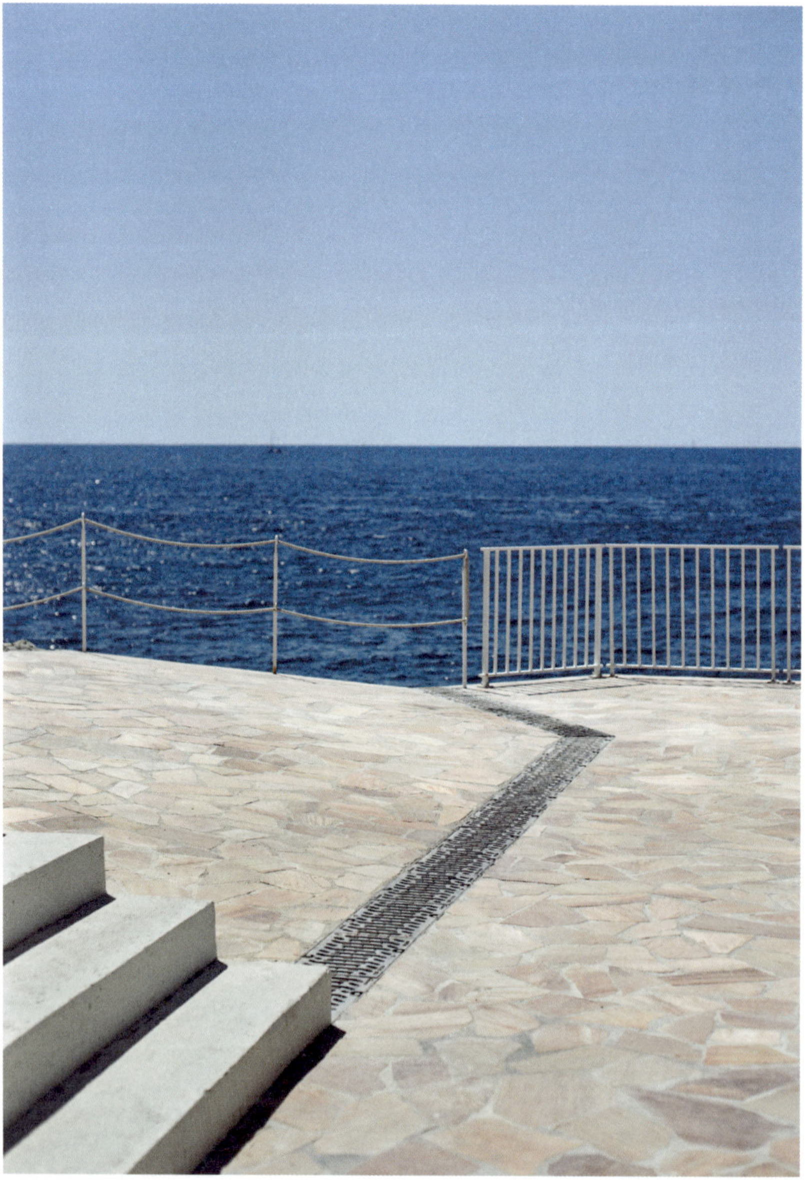

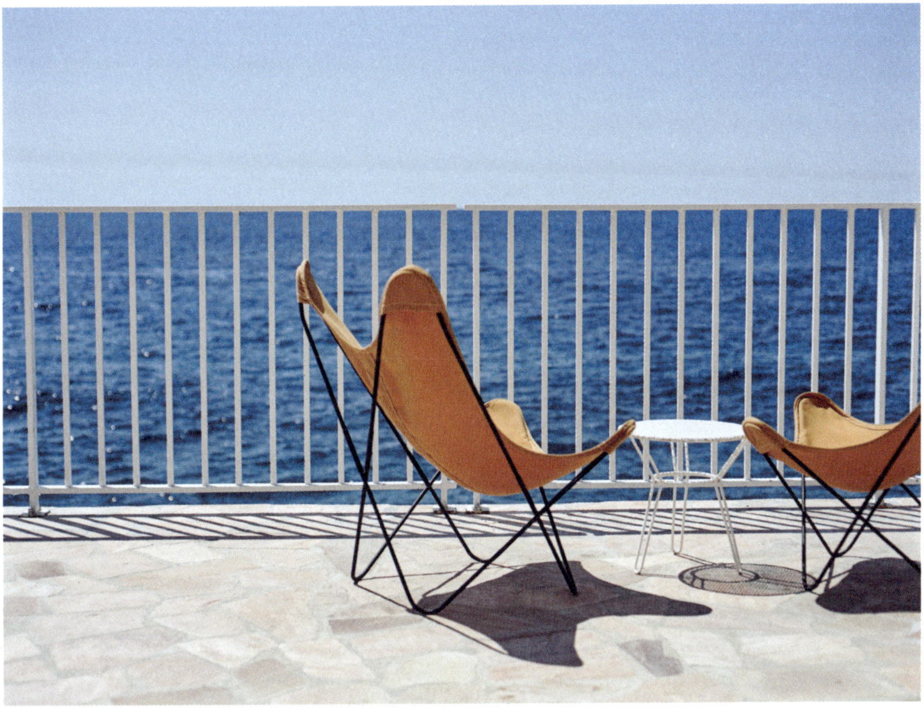

L'USINE HISTORIQUE, LES PARFUMERIES FRAGONARD

Museum

20 Boulevard Fragonard, 06130 Grasse
+33 (0)4 93 36 44 65
fragonard.com

Grasse is synonymous with scents and is known as the world's perfume capital. You are constantly reminded of this history as you walk around the streets of the old town with perfume shops and museums on every corner.

Fragonard is perhaps the best known of the perfume houses in Grasse, dating back to 1926 when the company was founded by Eugène Fuchs, an entrepreneur who named the brand after the Grasse-born painter Jean-Honoré Fragonard. Their historic, working factory and museum have remained in the family ever since and provide a beautiful place to visit while in town.

After you've learnt about the floral history of the region, book a short perfumery class to learn the basics of perfume making. You will blend different smells before concocting your own scent to take away.

Fragonard
he. Carvi
Fragonard
he. Bergamote
Fragonard
he. Camomille
Romaine Anjou
Fragonard

BOULEVARD
FRAGONARD

FONDATION MARGUERITE ET AIMÉ MAEGHT

Museum

623 chemin des Gardettes, 06570 Saint-Paul-de-Vence, near Vence
+33 (0)4 93 32 81 63
fondation-maeght.com

As you drive up the winding hill to the medieval town of Saint-Paul-de-Vence, you pass one of Provence's most captivating museums. The Maeght Foundation was opened in 1964 and is a unique architectural complex displaying modern and contemporary art across all disciplines.

The white, avant-garde building was designed by the Catalan architect Josef Lluís Sert, who was passionate about bringing modernity to the Mediterranean. The serene but innovative structure is as much of an artwork as many of the pieces it houses.

As well as showing thematic temporary exhibitions, the foundation has a large permanent collection, which features important works by Alexander Calder, Georges Braque, Alberto Giacometti and Marc Chagall.

The sculpture garden surrounding the museum is perhaps the most magical part of the Maeght experience, with Miró mosaics, Braque stained glass and Barbara Hepworth's elusive abstract sculpture to name a few highlights.

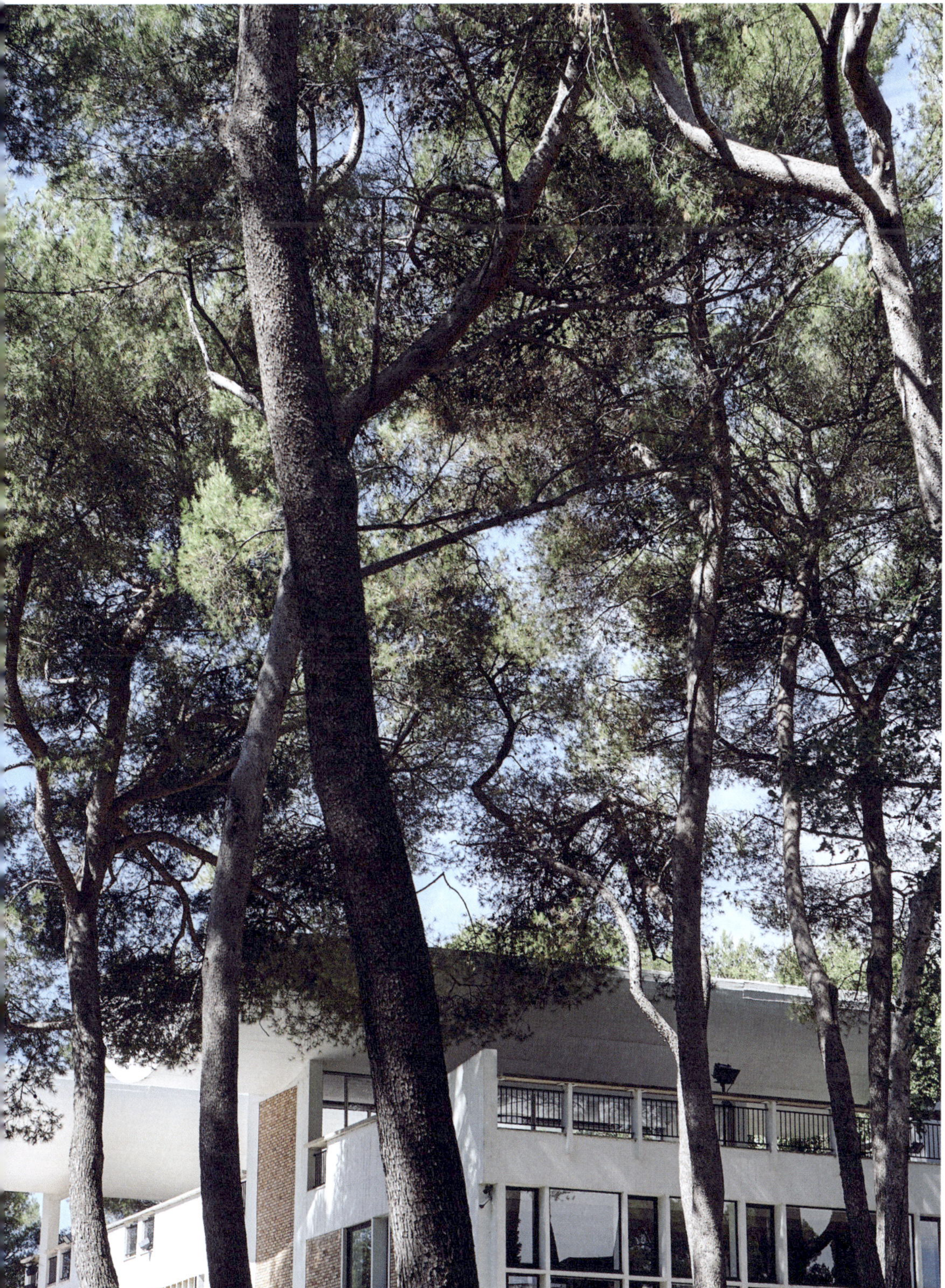

MUSÉE PICASSO

Museum

Place Mariejol, 06600 Antibes
+33 (0)4 92 90 54 28

Perched on the seafront at Antibes, the Picasso Museum is worth visiting for both the artwork and the sea views. The building, Château Grimaldi, was built on the foundations of a Roman fort in the 16th century and was formerly the town hall.

Picasso used the château as a studio from July to December 1946. Subsequently the building held several exhibitions of Picasso's work, and in 1966 became the first Picasso Museum, dedicated to housing a substantial collection of the artist's work including the mythological Joie de Vivre and lots of his witty ceramics. The museum now also showcases the work of other, related artists. Head first to the ground floor terrace where sculptures by Germaine Richier are displayed overlooking the endless bright blue Mediterranean.

While in the area you can also see two monumental Picasso works at the small War and Peace Museum in Vallauris.

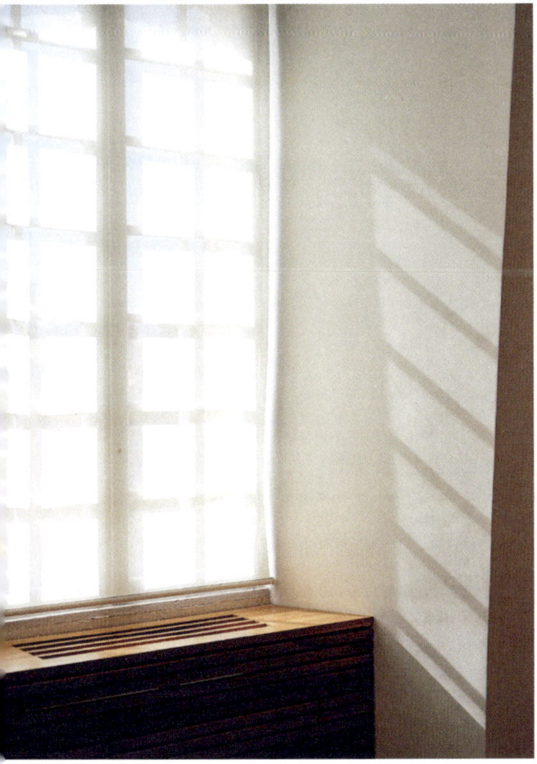

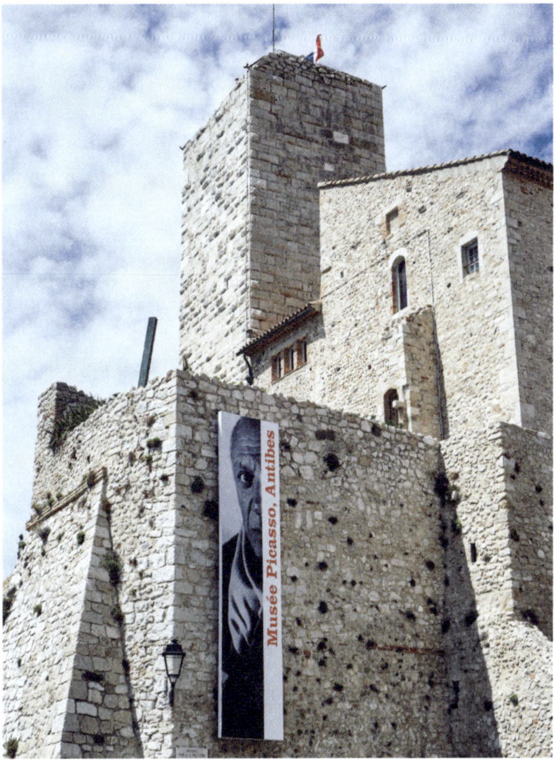
Musée Picasso, Antibes

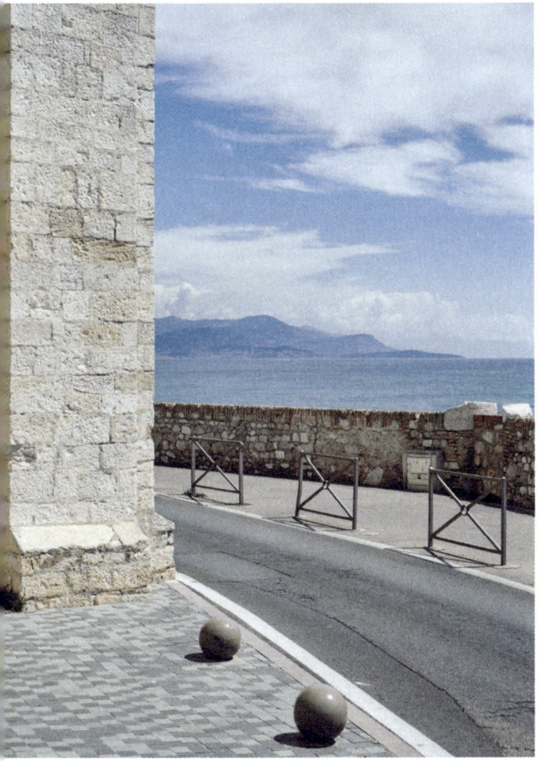

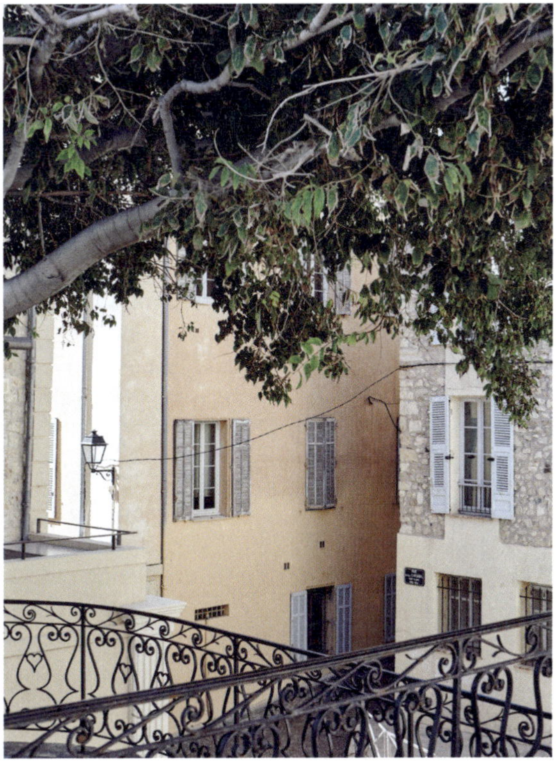

CAP MODERNE

Architectural Estate

Avenue de la Gare, 06190 Roquebrune Cap-Martin, near Menton
+33 (0)6 48 72 90 53
capmoderne.com

Roquebrune-Cap-Martin, between Menton and Monaco, is a strip of coast with unspoilt beaches and epic views. In the 1920s Eileen Gray, a pioneering modernist architect, fell in love with the region and decided to turn her talents to building a summer house here with her lover Jean Badovici.

Cap Moderne, as it is now known, opened to the public in 2015. It is a site of architectural importance featuring Eileen Gray's house, cryptically named Villa E-1027, and three other modernist properties built near to the main house. Villa E-1027 is a wonderfully striking white building featuring legendary Le Corbusier murals, restored original furniture and charming details by Eileen herself. Nearby, Le Cabanon is an enthralling addition, a small cabin beautifully designed by Le Corbusier, adjoined to the L'Étoile de Mer restaurant. Additionally, Le Corbusier built five holiday cabins, intended as a prototype of modular design.

To visit Cap Moderne you must pre-book a guided tour. They run twice a day in the warmer months and are available in a range of languages.

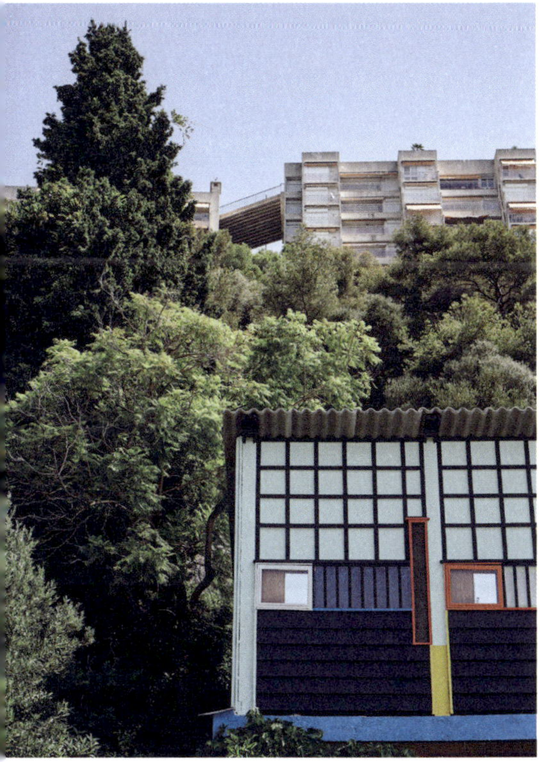
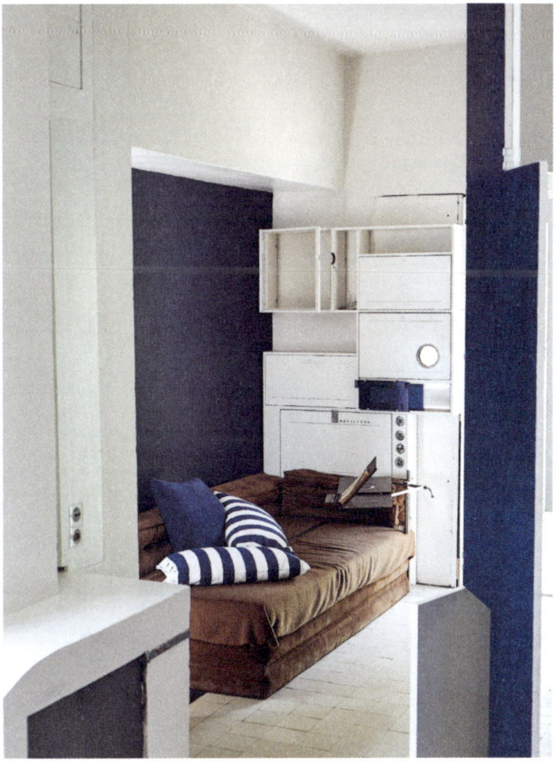
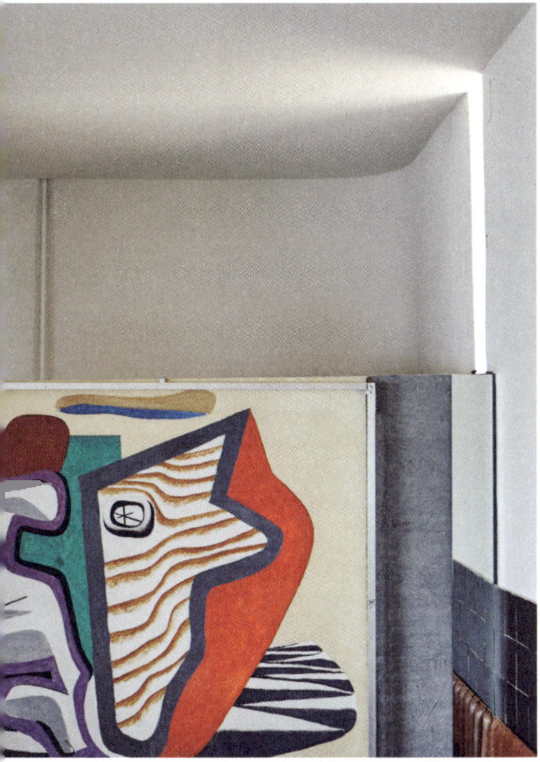
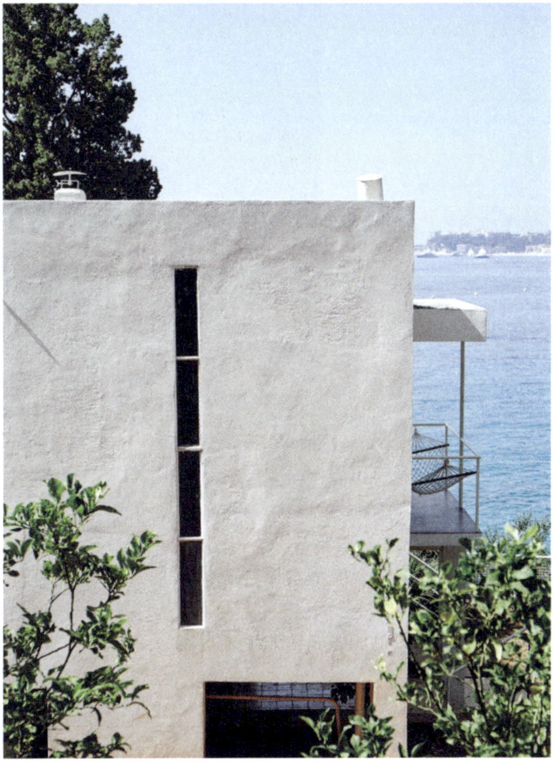

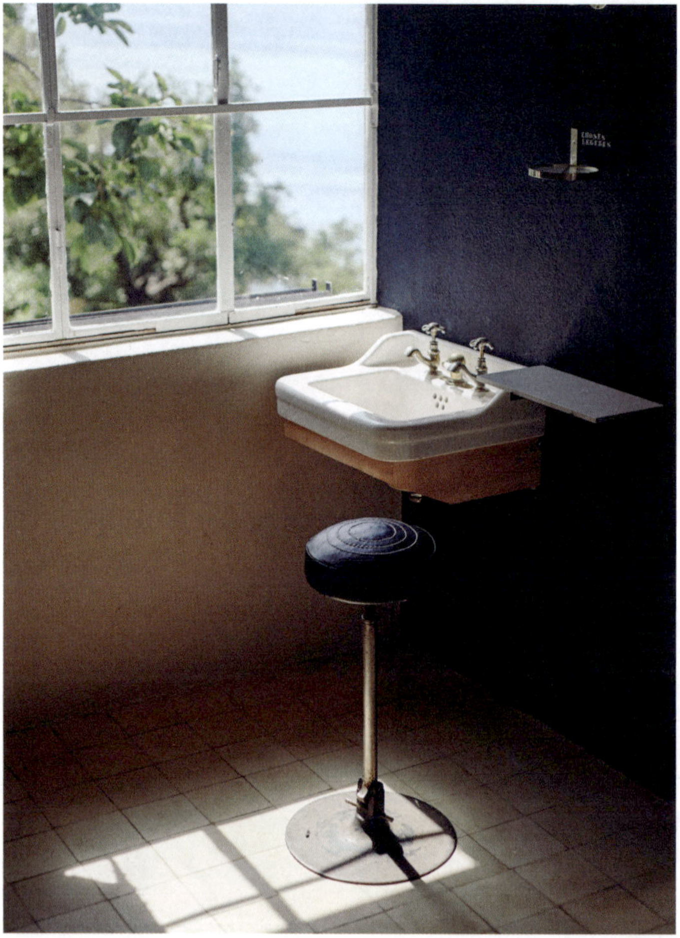

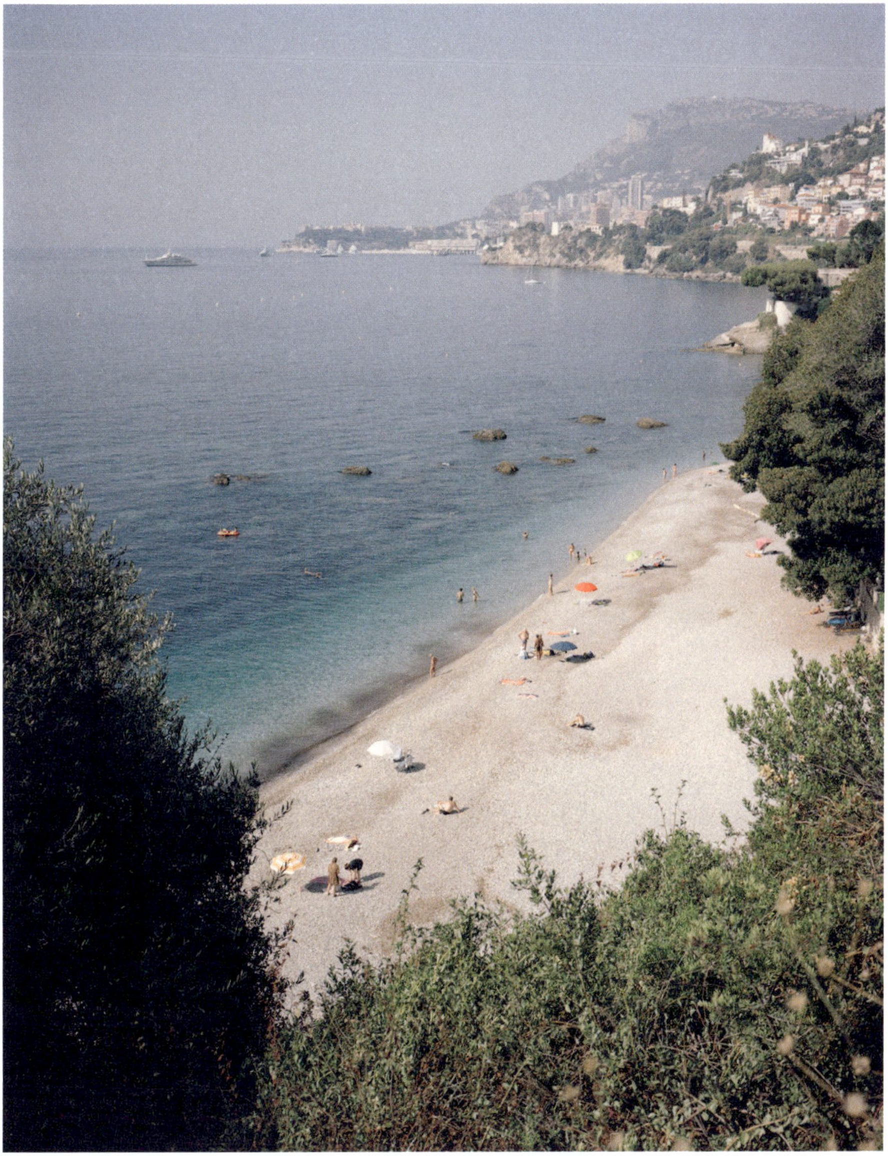

MIRAZUR

Restaurant

30 avenue Aristide Briand, 06500 Menton
+33 (0)4 92 41 86 86
mirazur.fr

Mauro Colagreco is regarded as one of the world's most talented and inspiring chefs.

After working with a number of 3 Michelin star chefs including Alain Passard and Alain Ducasse, he opened Mirazur in Menton in 2006. His Italo-Argentinian heritage provides some but not all of the character of his modern international style. The intricate dishes are an expression of his imagination and Mirazur is a place for him to play with flavours and obtain the most from the vibrant Provençal ingredients.

The restaurant is moments from the Italian border, with jaw-dropping views over the endless azure sea. The elegant dining room provides a serene but smart environment to maximise the food's appeal.

Menus are inspired by the sea, the mountains and the gardens. Signature dishes - such as Gillaredeau Oyster, cream of shallots and declination of William pears - rarely leave the menu, but other dishes change with the seasons.

Mirazur is always named as one of the world's top ten restaurants. A meal by Mauro is truly memorable; he captures the essence of Provence in an entirely new and exciting way.

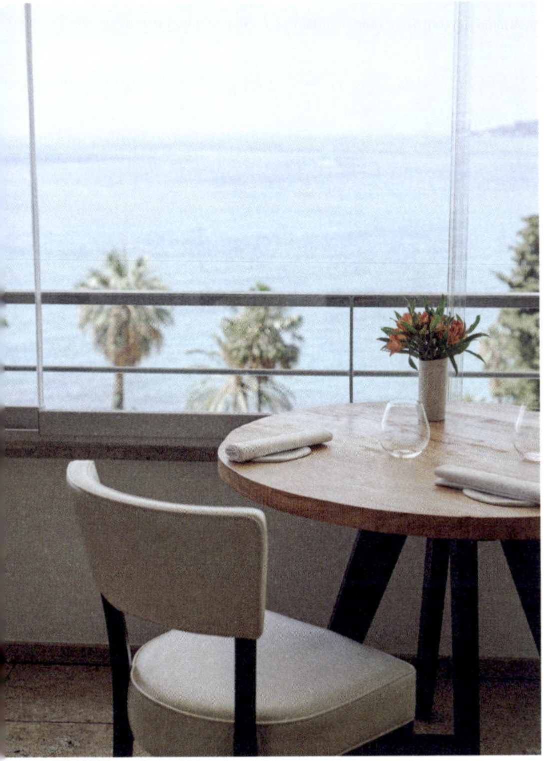

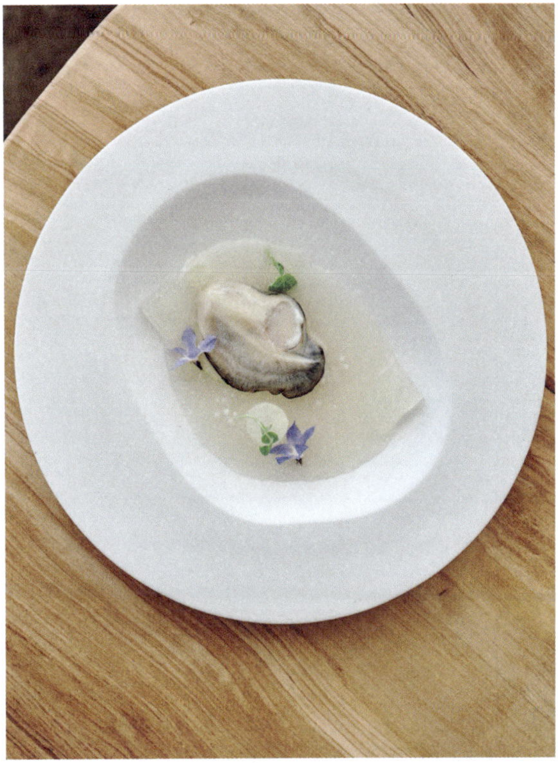

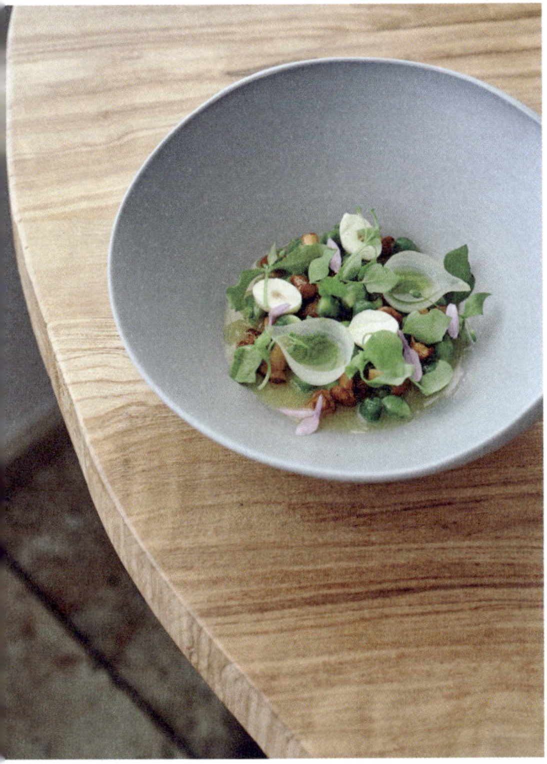

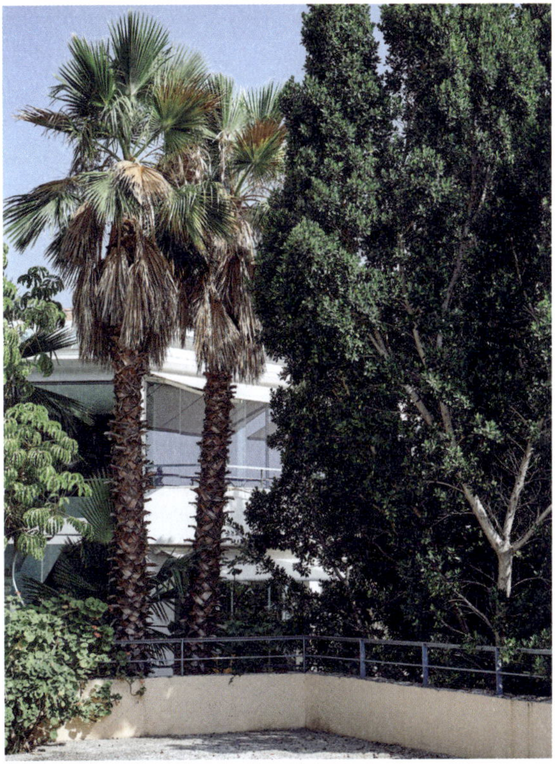

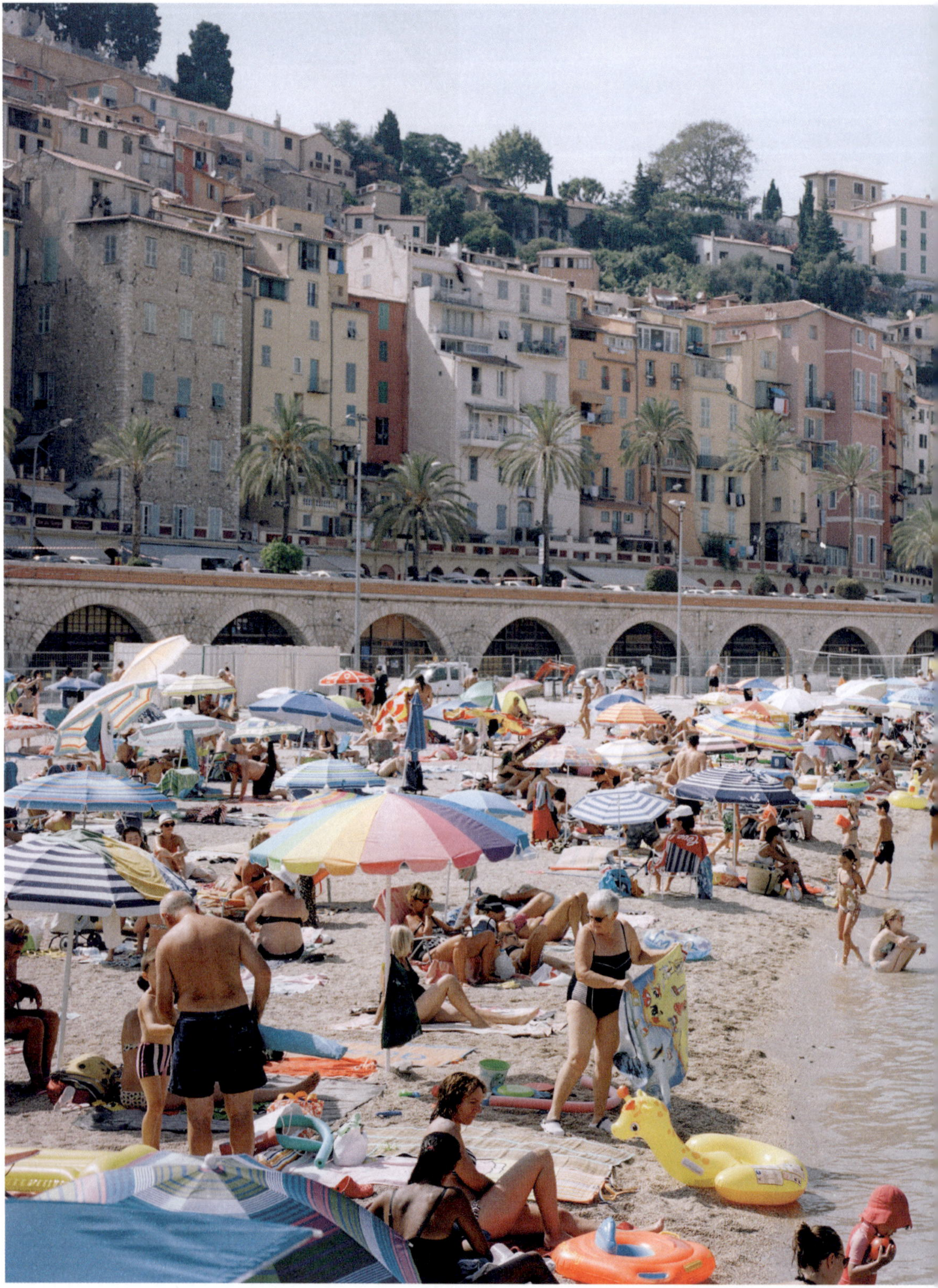

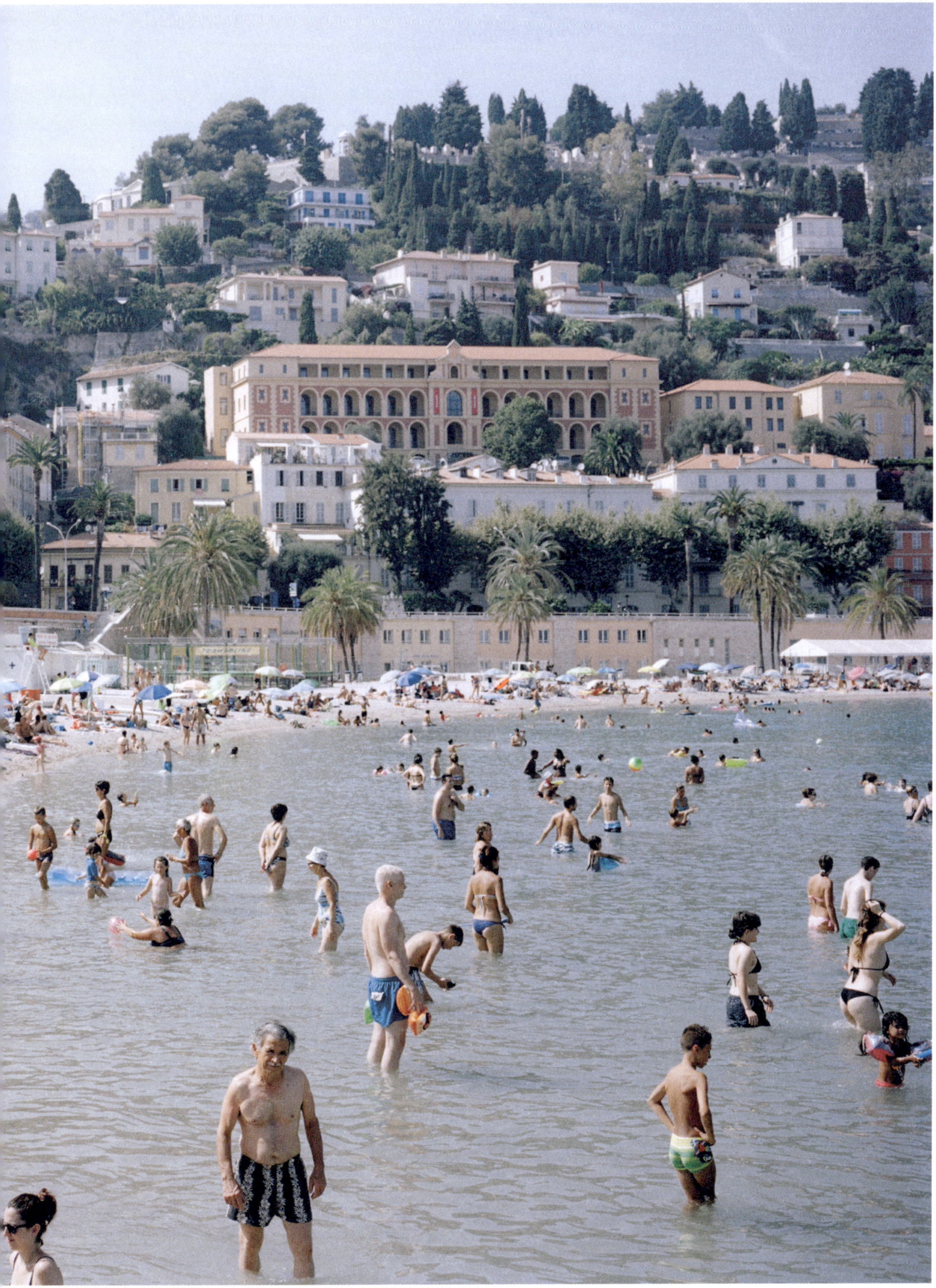

FRÉDÉRIC FEKKAI

BEAUTY INDUSTRY ENTREPRENEUR

Frédéric Fekkai is a global beauty industry entrepreneur and celebrity hairstylist. He was born and raised in Aix-en-Provence, and moved to New York at the age of 21 to start his career. After creating hairstyles for models on both catwalks and magazine covers, he opened two luxury salons in New York City before going on to launch his own line of hair care products. Frédéric has styled the hair of many prominent women, such as Kim Basinger, Sigourney Weaver, Claudia Schiffer, and Hillary Clinton.

In 2015, in partnership with his wife, Shirin von Wulffen, Frédéric acquired 'Côté Bastide', a 25-year-old lifestyle brand from his hometown of Aix-en-Provence. The couple re-launched the business as 'Bastide', a collection of natural beauty and luxury home products. The name is inspired by the couple's own Bastide (a Provençal manor house) in Aix.

Bastide is a collection of natural beauty products, all made in Provence by artisans with generations of expertise using potent Provence ingredients, and no toxins. Bastide's flagship store, in the heart of Aix, is popular with locals and visitors alike.

You are originally from Aix-en-Provence... what was it like growing up there?
Growing up in a city that is surrounded closely by one of the most beautiful countrysides (Le paysage de Cezanne) was both healthy and inspiring. Even to this date I am impressed by the beauty of the town's architecture, the golden light, the dolce vita and the scents.

Growing up in Aix-en-Provence there was a sense of easiness and it gave me an appreciation for time, culture and lifestyle. In short, it was a happy childhood upbringing.

And then you lived and worked for a while in New York... tell us about why you moved?
I originally moved to New York for a year to work for a French hair care company and fell instantly in love with the city and extended my stay. New York has taught me about business, helped my creativity to flourish and has broadened my experiences.

What brought you back to Provence?
As I was building my family I realised that my roots from Provence got more important to me and I wanted to share it.

The quality of Provençal life is a privilege; the air is healthy, the nature is so colourful, the local ingredients are of superior quality and I realised that beauty here comes from this way of life.

Tell us about your style and vision for Bastide.
When my wife and I bought Bastide we wanted to celebrate the magnificent Provençal region and its artisans. So we wanted to be 100% authentic, made in Provence with natural local ingredients.

And how do you choose the ingredients that go into your products?
The terroir of Provence gives us our palette, and we are fortunate to work with local artisan makers – we call them Beautisans – beauty

artisans – who have deep expertise. They have been working with these local ingredients for generations, and they have true savoir-faire. They know the land and how to get the best out of local ingredients, and which ingredients to use during which season. We never stray far from Provence. Being connected to the terroir and being authentic to the area are our priorities.

Which is your favourite product in the Bastide range and why?
I can't pick a favourite! We've spent so much time on them all that it is truly very hard to pick. Shirin's favourite is the Rose Olivier fragrance – the scent is completely special and inspired from a lunch we had in Grasse two summers ago.

Our kids love using the deep repair hand creams – the packaging is colourful and reminds them of their paint tubes. The formula is so safe, so we let them go wild using them.

What is it that you think makes Provence so special?
There is no place like it on earth. It is a land of beauty and Aix is a city of creativity. The streets are literally filled with artisans, painters, sculptors, musicians, chefs – there is passion and soul in their work, a human touch, and it is all perfectly imperfect.

The terroir here is so rich – the plants thrive, the way people live, eat, interact and love all slow down – they take the time to do it right. The air here is aromatic and intoxicating – the light is ethereal and exquisite, practically golden. Your senses are immediately seduced by the colours, textures and scents.

When I arrive in Aix, my shoulders just come down two centimetres.

So where are your favourite places to go in Provence?
I love spending time at the Château La Coste, a world class domaine, because it is so energising to arrive in a vineyard that has so much art and amazing epicurean estate.

Who is your greatest inspiration – in work and in life?
I love people in general, from all areas of the world - I get my inspiration from them. I also love to travel, to discover and watch movies and theatre. Let's not forget the museums and galleries all around the world.

What inspires me in life is some of my heroes who contribute to special causes such as fighting poverty, diseases and helping education.

Finally... Have you got a secret ingredient that has an unexpected use in terms of skincare?
Of course! But it is a secret that I cannot share at the moment as we are in the middle of development.

The only thing I will reveal is that it is critical and fundamental to all of our skin health, and it is the reason Aix-en-Provence came to be.

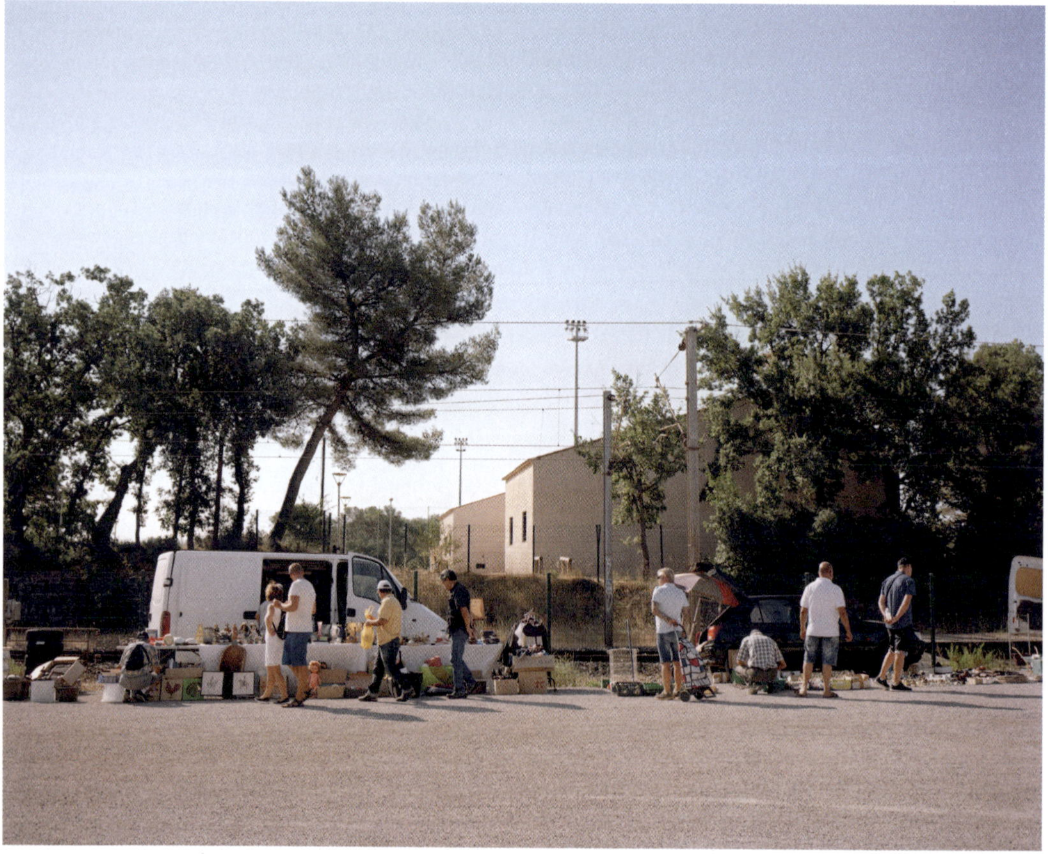

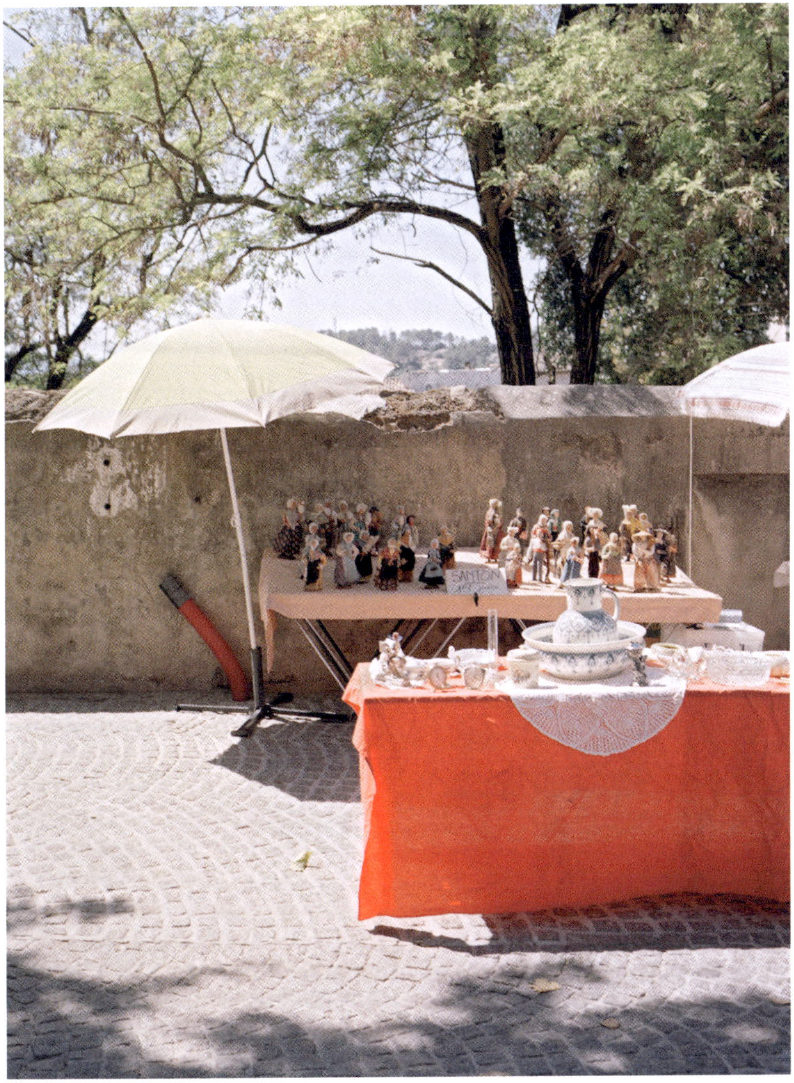
SANTON

MADELEINE HERBEAU

VINEYARD OWNER & DIRECTOR

Madeleine Herbeau is from the 4th generation of the Herbeau family to produce wine at Château Barbebelle. The land was first cultivated by the Romans, and in the 16th century a château was built that still stands today making it one of the oldest vineyards in Aix-en-Provence.

After studying business and working in Paris, Madeleine decided to join her father to help modernise the family business. Her father's experience, knowledge and techniques were essential to retain the quality and traditions of Château Barbebelle but she wanted to help bring the business into the 21st century so it could be passed on for generations to come.

Tell us your story and how you came to be part of the Château Barbebelle winery?
I was born as an only child at Château Barbebelle, a family estate for four generations. While I loved the Château and winemaking, I wanted to complete my studies to offer me maximum opportunities so that I had the choice whether or not to join my father at Barbebelle.

After business school (EDHEC) I worked for a year as a marketing manager at Nestlé but soon realised my real passion lay at Barbebelle so I left Paris and came back home. I now spend every day working with my father and also my fiancé at Château Barbebelle!

Winemaking is part of your family's tradition... what are your earliest memories of Barbebelle?
I have always been very lucky to live in this environment and when I was young I spent a lot of my time among the vines. Even when I was doing other activities with my father around the property like horse riding, we always had to find time to check the vines!

Tell us about your style and vision for Château Barbebelle.
Our vineyard is unique because of many things - the charm of the 16th century château, the terroir with the Trévaresse Mountain that gives us great 'argilo-calcaire' soil, and the cypress and oak trees. It's great for truffles, vines and wild animals and we have a lot of respect for the nature within the grounds. The property is 300 hectares in all, which is very rare near Aix-en-Provence, and only 45 hectares of the land is the vines.

We listen to the soil and our vines. We have vines up to 45 years old and only produce 50 hectolitres of wine as we respect the vines. We produce great wines with mostly Grenache and Syrah, but also Cinsault and Cabernet Sauvignon. We also don't use any chemicals or pesticides.

Our raison d'etre is to share our family business with the world. We have been a team for four generations and we know exactly how we each work. Château Barbebelle is more than a job; we work here but also live here. It is a passion and a lifestyle.

Nowadays, the potential to export is high so we have adjusted our marketing strategy to be a bit more modern while keeping the family traditions. I created a new label depicting a bearded man (Barbebelle means "beautiful beard") and this has helped put Château Barbebelle on the map.

And what is it that makes Provence so ideal for grape growing?
The terroir and the weather! We have good soil and all-year sun. Occasionally the winemakers have to adapt and water the vines, but most years we have the right amount of rainfall.

Why do you think Provençal rosé is having such a resurgence recently?
I think it's because of the Provençal lifestyle. People drink rosé on sunny days when they are having a good time!

Rosé from Provence is inimitable. You can find good red wines all over the world but the best rosé is in Provence – no doubt. We have the soil, the weather and the oenologists.

Furthermore, people love to drink rosé so they can reminisce or imagine being in Provence - near a fountain in the sun or surrounded by lavender fields!

How do you see Provence being represented in the international market?
Provence is very well represented in the market, both in terms of travel and wine. People enjoy their time here so come again and tell all their friends. And most people enjoy drinking Provençal wine while they are here too!

And what do you think makes Provence special?
The sun and the beautiful, charming little villages! Aix-en-Provence is a magnificent city and very representative of the region as a whole.

Where are your favourite places to go in Provence?
Calanque (the National Park between Marseille and Cassis) is beautiful! But I also love spending days in Aix-en-Provence, just wandering the streets and visiting the shops, restaurants and galleries.

Is there a winemaker in the region, or the world, that you admire?
My favourite winemaker in Provence is Château Pibarnon in Bandol. Château Sainte-Marguerite in Côtes de Provence is also great.

Internationally, I admire the success of Viña Marty in Chile!

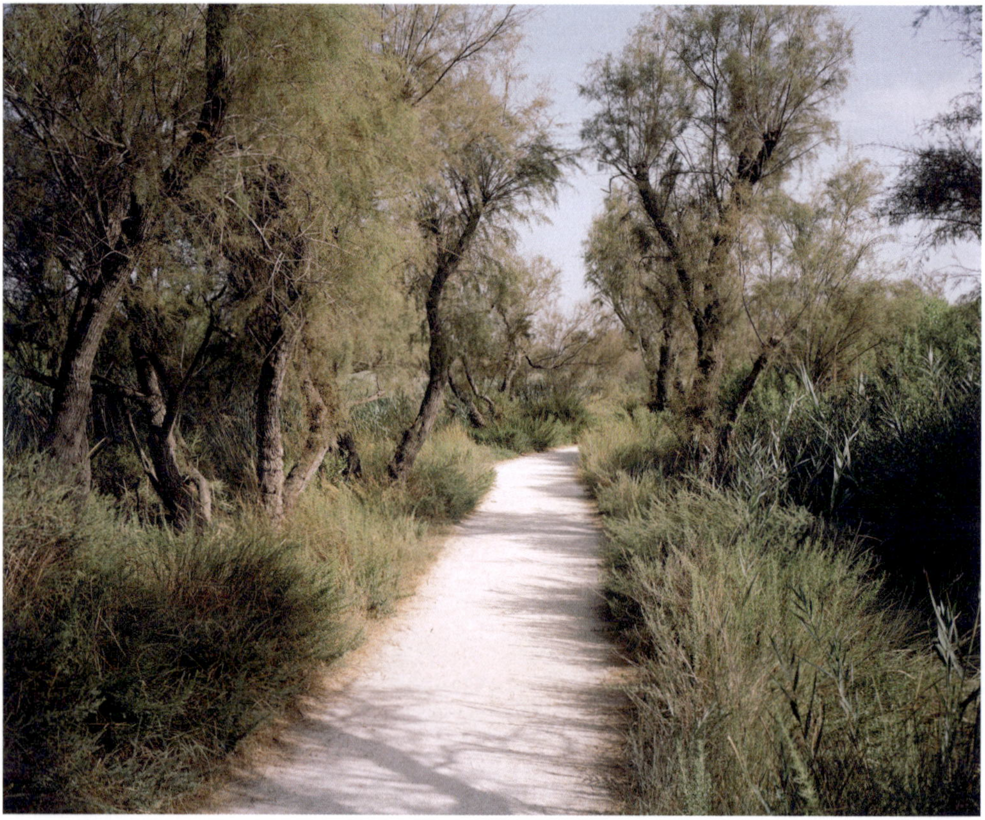

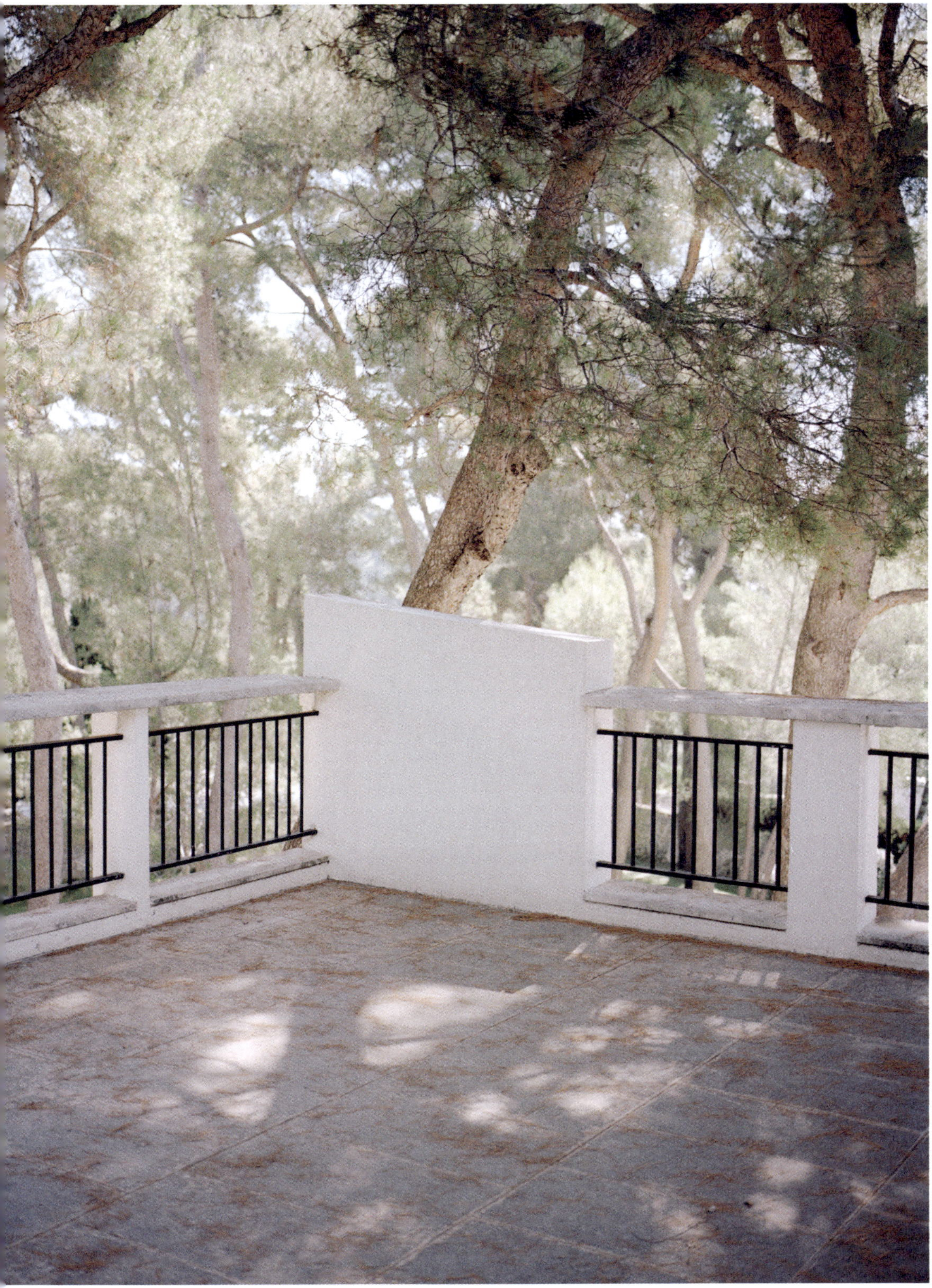

JAMIE BECK

PHOTOGRAPHER & INFLUENCER

Jamie Beck is a photographer and social media influencer who left New York in 2016 to spend a year focusing on personal work in Provence. She is most known for pioneering the Cinemagraph, a living photograph, with her creative partner Kevin Burg at their studio in lower Manhattan, Ann Street Studio. She has created international photography, video and cinemagraph campaigns for many well-known brands as well as contributing to publications around the world.

You aren't from Provence originally... where is home?
I spent 13 years in New York City, so I call myself a New Yorker. I certainly think like one! Originally though, I was born and raised in Texas. With all that said, I never really felt a true sense of "home" until I lived in Provence.

And when you arrived in Provence, what was your first impression?
All my senses were taken over. The way the air feels against your skin is so alive, your nose is intoxicated by the smell of the flowers and earth. There is a dustiness to the atmosphere that seems to blanket the passage of time... and then you look around and you see a symphony of colours. That is how I always know when I am in Provence, when the sky is royal blue over a sea of greens dotted by bursts of yellow, red, purple and pinks.

Tell us about your style and vision.
My style has changed a lot since moving to Provence. I think it is a reaction to all the colours after living in a black and white world in New York. There is not a distinction between what is happening in my photographic work and how I am living my life. I sort of am my work. Provence opened up a world of nature to me I have never known. There is a natural rhythm of life here that is perfectly balanced, that you fit into and instantly understand. My vision has shifted and continues so to reflect this awe of nature I am now abiding by. As I experience each character the seasons bring, I equate it to the human experience and our mortality.

A lot of your photographs imply a narrative or appear to include symbols... is this something specific or just an atmosphere?
It has become very important to me for my work to have symbolic meaning. I do not speak publicly to what these things represent because I like for people to project their own conscience into my work, what it means to them and their life experiences. Living among the rhythm of nature I have become very in-tune with my own human experiences and able to feel and create based around this with subtle gestures or props telling my life story.

What is normally the starting point for a new photograph?
An emotion, a new piece of fruit from the market, whatever is blooming in my garden... I live in the present each day and let inspiration come from what is happening in that moment. Sometimes, I have an idea that I cannot execute right away, such as my reinterpretation of Leonardo da Vinci's "Last Supper", so I will become obsessed with it in my mind, going over all the detailed plans until I can create it.

Your photos have a very painterly quality, which artists/photographers inspire you?
The light in France is like nowhere else on earth.

I think I could strive to create the same concepts and style in other places around the world but you cannot recreate the French light which I believe gives it that painterly quality. Over the years, the photographers whose work I admire shifts as my focus changes.

Right now, I am very inspired by Irving Penn's work just because I appreciate the artistic struggle to construct a still life that is both visually pleasing and meaningful symbolically. He was such a master in that regard. Mostly though, in a world that is now overwhelmed by imagery, I have been looking more to painters for inspiration.

Photography now moves so quickly it feels as if people are not stopping to think, to create, to worry about the details. The details of a Dutch painting by Jan Davidsz de Heem are unmatched photographically, they are such a celebration of life it brought tears to my eyes. The intense drama of a Caravaggio painting communicated through light and shadow is three-dimensional. As I have learned to slow down to the pace of Provence, I have also learned to slow down how I create, to make less work with more meaning. Of course, you cannot help but love the work of Cézanne, Van Gogh, Matisse, or Renoir while living in Provence because you are walking through their fields, their flowers, their picnics, their paintings; understanding it in a whole new perspective.

So what do you think makes Provence special?
It is the culture of Provence that makes it what it is. The way the people preserve their way of life so it may continue as it always has been. It's wonderfully unfussy, unpretentious, quiet, and natural. The seasonal foods that come weekly to the market from the nearby farms are a way of life, and it is the same with the wine. You are free from so much noise now created in the world when you enter Provence, your mind is clear and all of a sudden your thoughts open up.

Where are your favourite places to go in Provence?
I love Arles! Great food, mysterious culture, incredible history, wonderful photography exhibitions. I love to bike through the Luberon on the trail where you can really experience the countryside. The view from Ménerbes is amazing as is the view of Gordes. Dinner at Le Mas Tourteron or La Bastide de Marie is always a magical treat for the tastebuds. Walking around Bonnieux enjoying the architecture when the autumn fête happens. I love to take a picnic to Château La Coste and watch classic films under the stars in the vineyard on their movie nights, or go to Lourmarin to listen to a piano concert at the Château. The best moments in Provence however, are when you get together with friends at one of their homes to share a home cooked meal. That is the real Provence.

And where do you shop for photography props, and what do you look for in particular?
The brocantes! I always check out the signs at the entrance of towns to see when the next brocante or vide grenier is – you can get the best regional props at the most inexpensive prices. Of course, every Sunday in L'Isle-sur-la-Sorgue there is a great brocante for prop shopping. As far as brick and mortar stores, La Maison d'Inès in Apt is one of my go-to spots.

Who is your greatest inspiration – in work and in life?
Georgia O'Keeffe. Her body of work, the photographic artefacts of her life, her approach to fashion and the way she lived and worked in the country I find so harmonious. She never let being a woman define how she wanted to live, but at the same time created work only possible through the perspective of a woman.

And lastly... what would be your dream commission?
My current dreams would be to do a project for the New York City Ballet, to see my work in a museum, and to film a movie.

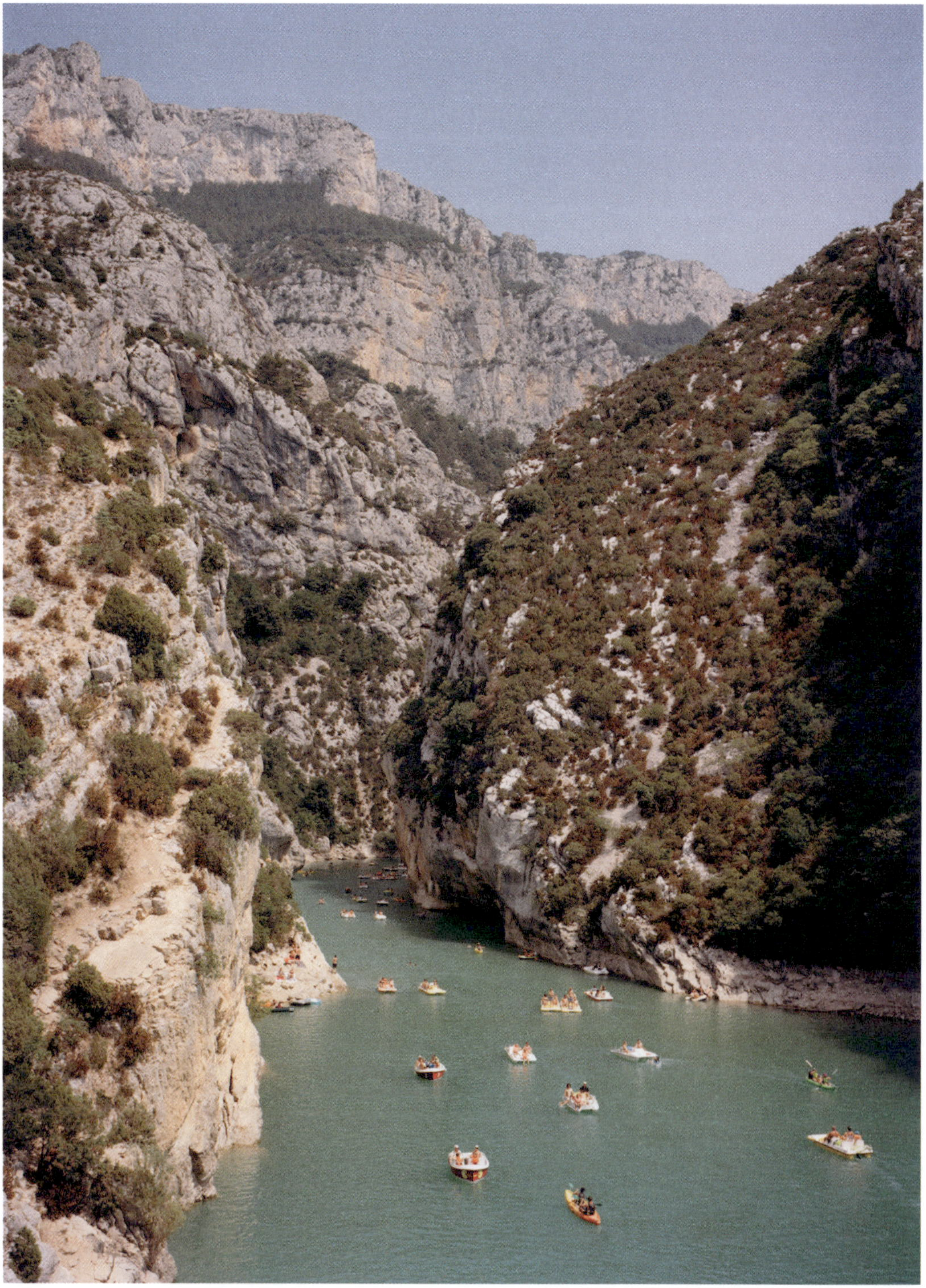

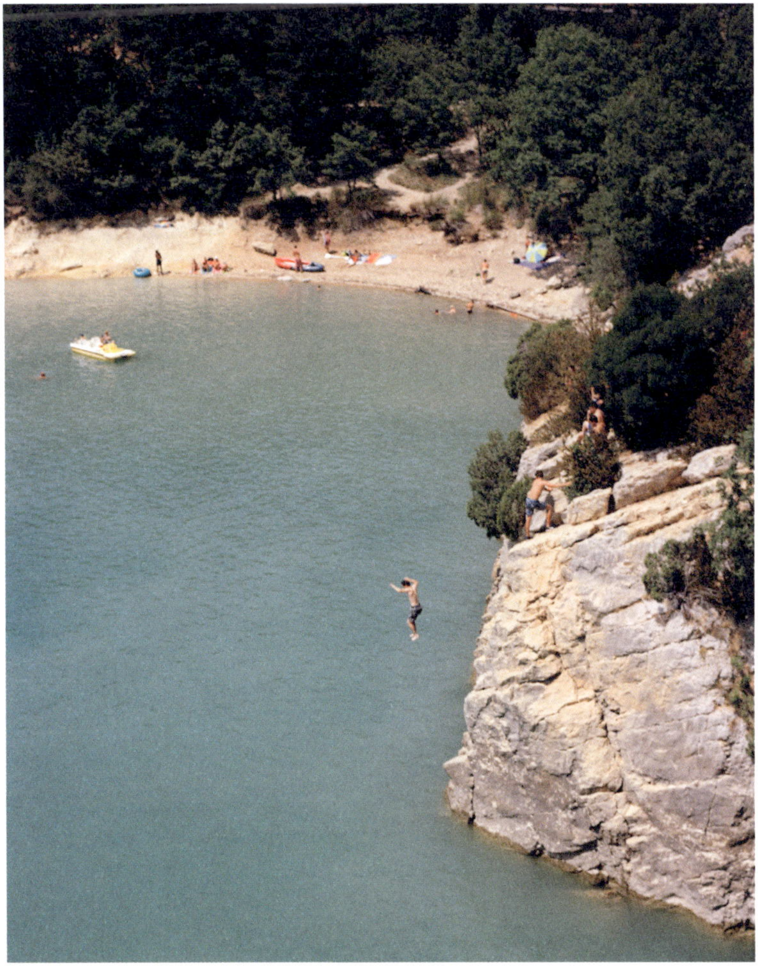

MAURO COLAGRECO
CHEF

Mauro Colagreco is the chef-owner of Mirazur restaurant in Menton. After training in Argentina, he moved to France in 2001 where he trained under Bernard Loiseau. He moved on to work in Paris with a number of 3 Michelin-star chefs including Alain Ducasse at the Hotel Plaza Athénée and Alain Passard at l'Arpège.

In 2006, Mauro decided to open his own restaurant and Mirazur was born. The following year he received his first Michelin star. Mirazur and Mauro have since garnered many more awards including Gault Millau's Chef of the Year 2009 (the first non-French chef to receive this title), a second Michelin star in 2012 and 4th place in the San Pellegrino World's 50 Best in 2017.

Mauro also owns Carne, a hamburger chain in Argentina, a brasserie in Paris called Grand Cœur, and is Executive Chef of AZUR restaurant in Beijing.

What's your story and why did you come to Provence?
It's quite unusual… I decided that I wanted to cook when I was 20 years old, which is considered a late beginning in the industry. Sometimes a crisis can be dangerous but sometimes it's a blessing and leads to a great opportunity! In fact, when I had to decide what I first wanted to do as a job, I was confused, I couldn't find my way. I tried to follow in my dad's footsteps as an accountant, but as with every job you must find passion in what you do and this wasn't the case here. I also tried to pursue a literary career, but that wasn't for me either.

It was my sister who reminded me of the pleasure and happiness I used to feel when I was a child, when I used to cook with my grandmother. That memory turned out to be a real journey back to rediscovering myself and my true passion. Cooking is what I am; I could not be anything else.

I think Menton is a very unique place. Mirazur is set on the Italian-French border, and we use ingredients from local markets on both sides which gives a fantastic selection of fresh produce. Behind us we have mountains and in front of us is the Mediterranean Sea. Our cuisine is about that, about borders, about capturing the best products of each culture, which I think is why I was so drawn to Menton. Cooking is also about reflecting the people of the regions and my aim is to show this by supporting local producers. Menton couldn't be more perfect for me. I feel that I have freedom here, and freedom is the base of creativity.

How do you define your style of cuisine?
My inspirations come from the environment surrounding me, the mountains, the sea and my garden – being on the Italian-French Border of the Côte d'Azur, this is perfect! If I had to choose some keywords to describe my cuisine they would be 'beauty', 'unexpected flavours' and 'sharing'. Eating is not just a physical need; food is what we are made of. We choose the food that we introduce in our body, it's

something so intimate and what we initially choose all comes down to sight. I try to couple flavours that mutually enhance each other to create unexpected tasting explosions, bringing traditional ingredients together in unique ways and celebrating the culinary landscape of Menton.

Do you think it is possible to make modern Provençal food successful while staying true to the traditions?
My philosophy is all about using the freshest and highest quality ingredients and allowing them to speak for themselves, rather than hiding the flavours with fancy techniques. We're lucky here in Menton to have wonderful produce - from markets in France and Italy – that is incredibly fresh and tastes of the sunshine. On the border between the two countries there is a special microclimate... It's unlike anywhere else.

When I'm coming up with a new dish, I think of it as a way of showcasing that ingredient in a different way, based on what is growing in my garden and what is in season.

What do you want people to feel while experiencing one of your meals?
I try to make something that works perfectly together and to challenge and excite my guests. People travel to Mirazur to discover the range of flavours from this region, and I hope to bring the essences of the Côte d'Azur on a plate.

And how important is presentation to you?
Very important, eating is about taste and smell, but of course it's also about the visual.

So crockery, cutlery and serving equipment must be important to you too... how do you choose it?
I choose it all myself, either on my travels or when I have a dish in my mind. I try to find the perfect chinaware and equipment to enhance the dish.

How have you seen Provence change in the time you've been here?
It hasn't changed too much! Menton is a place that doesn't change a lot and needs a lot of time to accept small changes. When I arrived in the town it was not easy, 10 years later people are now proud to have a gastronomic restaurant but I had to work a lot in order to make it happen.

Are there any up and coming chefs or restaurants in Provence that you're particularly excited about?
I very much like Alexandre Mazzia's restaurant; he does excellent work. And of course Gérald Passédat (of Le Petit Nice in Marseille and Louison at Villa La Coste in Aix-en-Provence) – he is a great friend with a beautiful and historic place that everybody visiting the area should try.

Who or what are your biggest influences?
The biggest influence is my surroundings – the Mediterranean Sea, the mountains, my garden, and the environment in Menton. It's such a rich melting pot of cultures and ingredients... the countryside, the surrounding Italian and French villages, the sea... this is what influences me most of all. I also take inspiration from my heritage - an Argentinian chef with family from Italy and Spain is quite unusual!

If you could have one meal anywhere... where would it be?
I think if I could go back in time, it would be back in Argentina in my grandparents' house. With my grandmother cooking for the family – she was a wonderful cook and I can still remember the smell of her kitchen.

And finally... if you were on a desert island and only allowed three ingredients, what would you take?
Wine, seeds and fresh water.

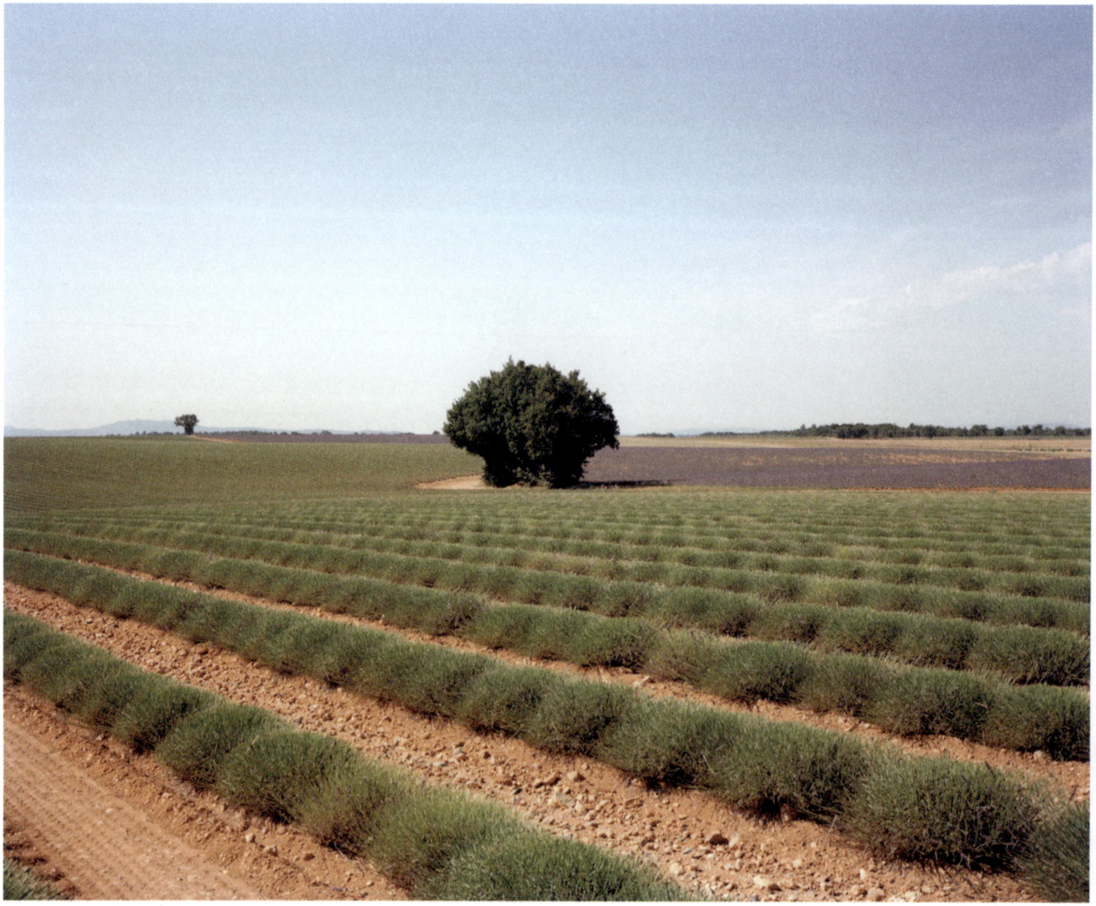

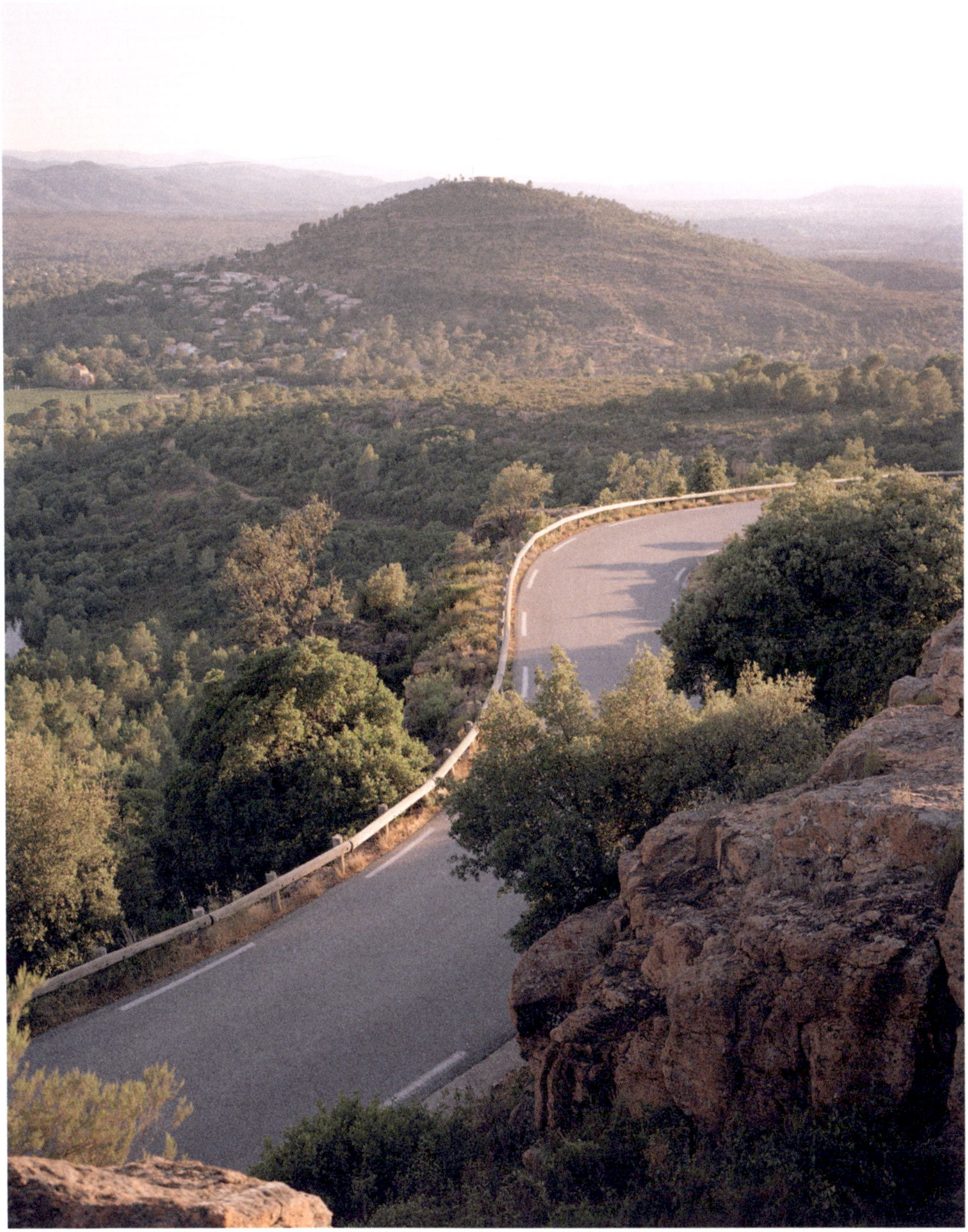

FURTHER IDEAS

AU VERRE LEVÉ
Wine bar and shop specialising in organic
and natural artisan wines.
15 rue Granet, 13100 Aix-en-Provence
+33 (0)4 86 31 08 15
auverreleve.com

DOMAINE SAINTE LUCIE & DOMAINES DES DIABLES
Second-generation family vineyard in the foothills
of Montagne Sainte-Victoire.
Chemin de la Colle, 13114 Puyloubier, near Aix-en-Provence
+33 (0)6 81 43 94 62
mip-provence.com

FONDATION VINCENT VAN GOGH ARLES
Modern museum displaying a selection of Van Gogh's pictures
alongside works by artists he has inspired.
35 ter, rue du Docteur-Fanton, 13200 Arles
+33 (0)4 90 93 08 08
fondation-vincentvangogh-arles.org

HOTEL CRILLON LE BRAVE
Stylish, luxury 36 room hilltop hotel with
a gastronomic restaurant.
Place de l'Eglise, 84410 Crillon le Brave, near Avignon
+33 (0)4 90 65 61 61
crillonlebrave.com

AU POT DE VIN
Wine bar and restaurant run by former 2 Michelin star chef Jean-Pierre Vila.
20 rue Commandant Vidal, 06400 Cannes
+33 (0)4 93 68 66 18
aupotdevin.com

MUSÉE BONNARD
The first museum in the world dedicated to the intimate art of Pierre Bonnard.
16 Boulevard Sadi Carnot, 06110 Le Cannet, near Cannes
+33 (0) 4 93 94 06 06
museebonnard.fr

CHÂTEAU DU ROUËT
Fifth-generation vineyard with a grand holiday house and separate cottages.
D47 route de Bagnols, 83490 Le Muy, near Draguignan
+33 (0)4 94 99 21 10
chateau-du-rouet.com

LA BASTIDE DE MARIE
18th century, boutique hotel and gastronomic restaurant, surrounded by 37 acres of vineyards.
64 chemin des Peirelles, 84560 Menerbes, Luberon
+33 (0)4 90 72 30 20
labastidedemarie.com

COOGEE
An antique-cluttered café with a terrace, serving speciality coffee and small plates.
100 Boulevard Baille, 13005 Marseille
+33 (0)6 86 57 52 55

LACAILLE
Friendly, modern French bistro owned by local couple, Alexis and Antonia Kloniecki.
42 rue des 3 Mages, 13006 Marseille
+33 (0)9 86 33 20 33

LE POULPE
Stylish seafood restaurant overlooking the port of Marseille.
84 Quai du Port, 13002 Marseille
+33 (0)4 95 09 15 91
lepoulpe-marseille.com

LA COMPAGNIE MARSEILLAISE
Provençal scents made by Jean-Pierre Brunet, inspired by the Marseille coastline.
36 rue Caisserie, 13002 Marseille
+33 (0)4 86 97 63 12
compagnie-marseillaise.com

DOMAINE LA COURTADE
83-acre vineyard spread over hills and plains
on the island of Porquerolles.
Île de Porquerolles, 83400 Hyères, near Toulon
+33 (0)4 94 58 31 44
lacourtade.com

LA COLOMBE D'OR
World-famous hotel and restaurant visited by artists
including Picasso, Matisse and Braque.
1 place du Général de Gaulle, 06570 Saint-Paul-de-Vence, near Vence
+33 (0)4 93 32 80 02
la-colombe-dor.com

LA CHAPELLE DU ROSAIRE
Unique chapel designed and constructed
by Henri Matisse.
466 avenue Henri Matisse, 06140 Vence
+33 (0)4 93 58 03 26
chapellematisse.com

LA POTERIE DU SOLEIL
Family-owned ceramics shop housed in an
original 18th century pottery.
373 route de Draguignan, 83690 Villecroze, near Draguignan
+33 (0)4 94 67 52 42
poterie-du-soleil.com

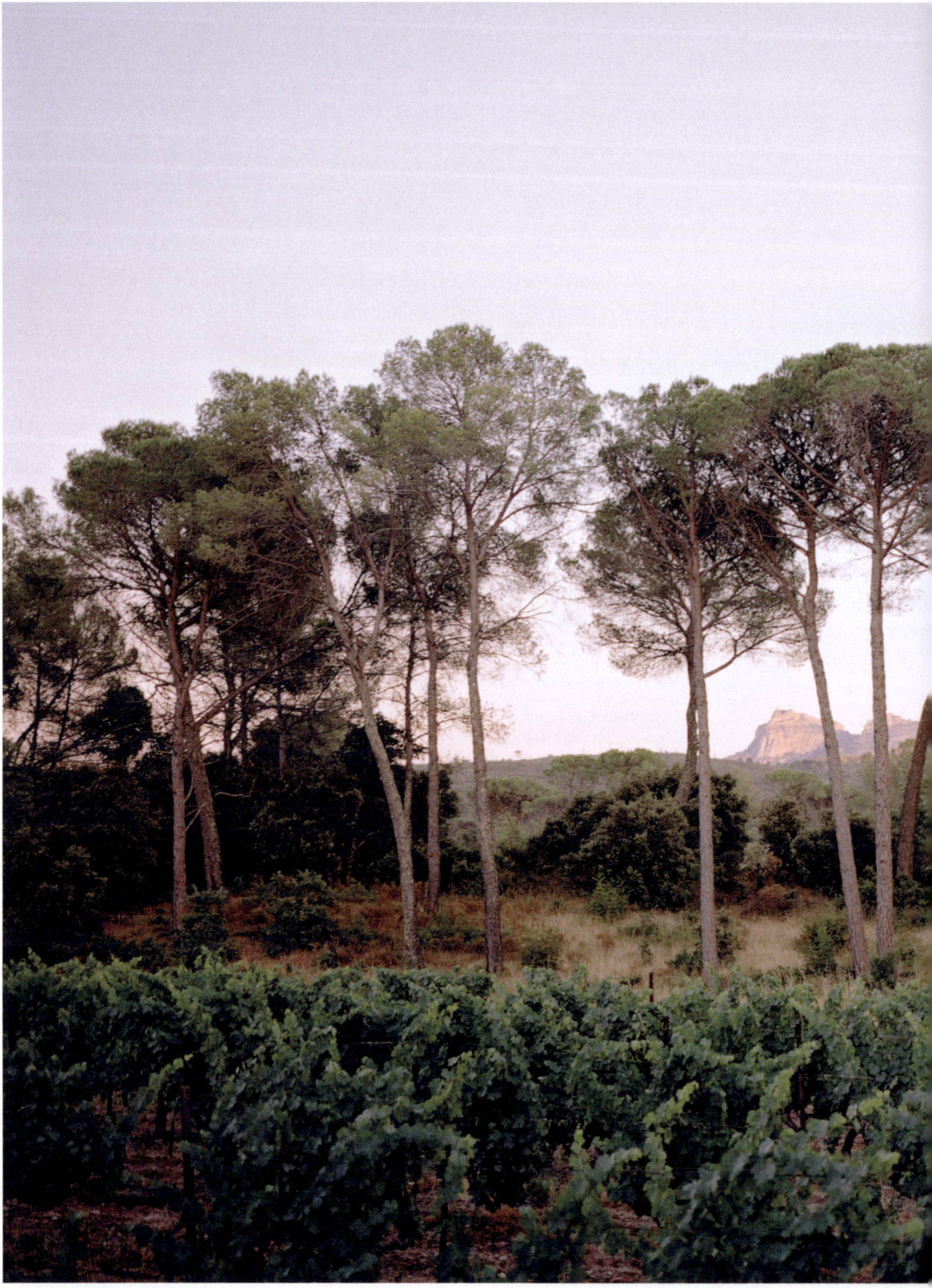

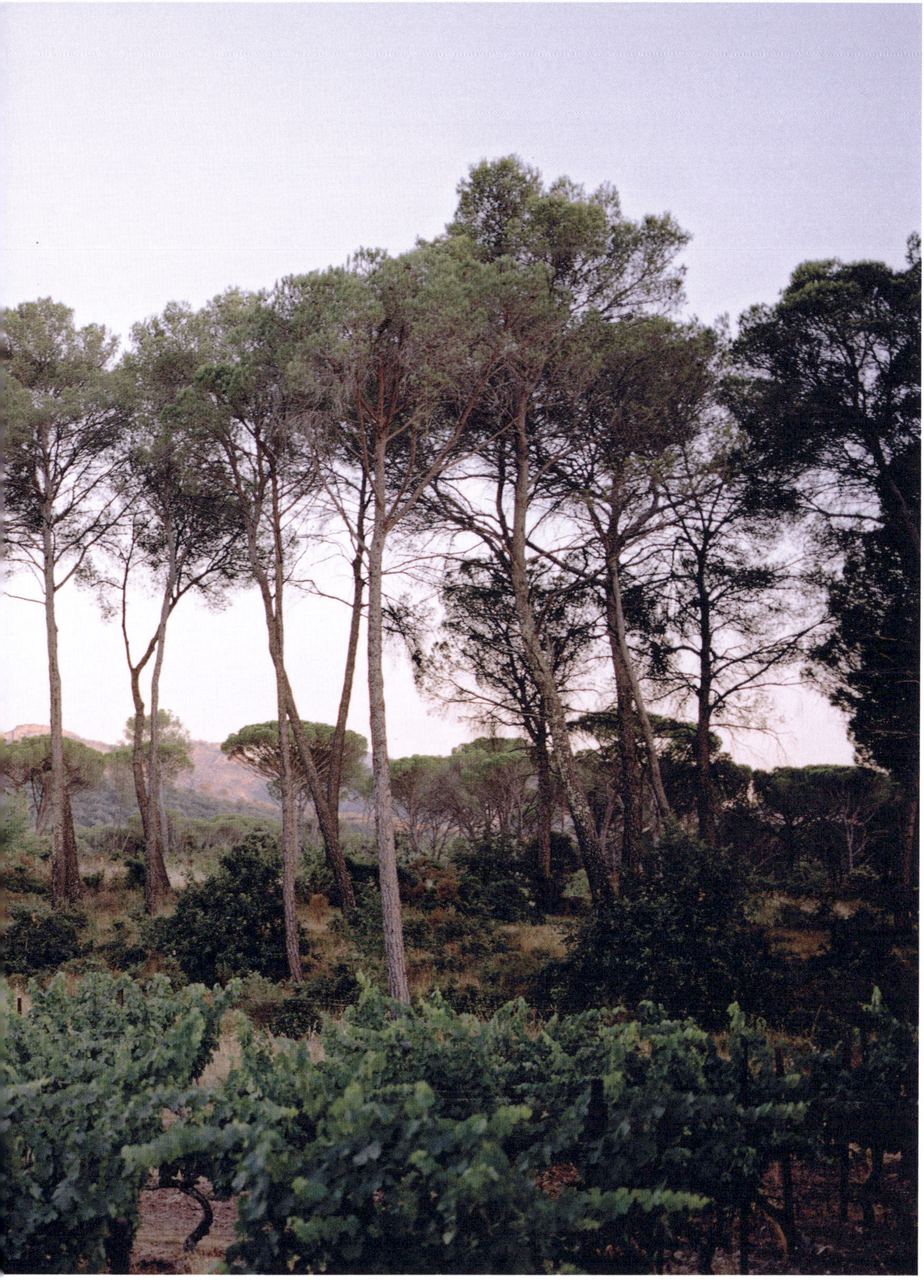

WEEKEND JOURNALS

Editor: Milly Kenny-Ryder
thoroughlymodernmilly.com

Designer: Simon Lovell

Photographer: Gabriel Kenny-Ryder
gabrielkennyryder.com

All venues have been visited personally.

Thank you to Jackie and John for everything you do for us,
and to Chris and Mark for your patient eyes.

First published in the United Kingdom in 2017 by Weekend Journals Ltd.

© Weekend Journals Ltd

All rights reserved. All text and images are exclusive to Weekend Journals Ltd and may not be reproduced or transmitted in any form or by any means, in part or in whole for any use without prior written permission.

Copyright Information:
p. 57-59 © atelier de Cézanne;
p. 63 (Bottom-right) Tadao Ando, Pavilion "Four Cubes to contemplate our environment";
p. 101-102 © FLC/ ADAGP, Paris and DACS, London 2017.

Printed by Taylor Bros Bristol Ltd on FSC approved uncoated paper
ISBN: 978-1-9998591-0-7

hello@weekendjournals.co.uk
weekendjournals.co.uk